GEOFF THOMPSON

Everything that Happens to Me is Good

summersdale

EVERYTHING THAT HAPPENS TO ME IS GOOD

Summersdale Publishers Ltd
46 West Street
Chichester
West Sussex
PO19 1RP
UK

www.summersdale.com

Printed and bound in Great Britain

ISBN: 1-84024-597-2
ISBN 13: 978-1-84024-597-4

As always, with big love and thanks to my beautiful wife Sharon for carrying my bones over some tough terrain.

Thank you to my lovely friend Margaret Ring for being an inspiration to me and my children over many a McDonald's coffee.

Also by Geoff Thompson

Contents

Foreword

Although I am primarily a writer of books and films, over the years I have also penned a bevy of articles for newspapers, magazines and my website. After many requests from readers (and several prompts from Richard Barnes, my friend and web master) I have decided to collect my favourites into the book you have before you now. I've also added a few extended and revised extracts from my book *The Elephant and the Twig* because they fit the ethos of this work. I personally love an uplifting article on the commute to work or a cerebral snack over lunch. (And whatever you do, don't give me a book to read in the loo – I might never come out again.)

There is something very satisfying and enjoyable (I think) about filling one of life's many stolen or idle moments with a good, quick read.

I hope this proves to be just that.

Geoff Thompson

Chapter 1

Be Nice

I read a fabulous poem once that has always stuck with me, not because it is sweet, rather because it is true. The poem went, 'I knew a man they called him mad the more he gave the more he had.'

I think we can assume from this small ditty that the man in question was a nice man who had stumbled upon one of life's great secrets: What you give out will return.

There is a massive profit in being nice, as long as you are not being nice for profit. And yet the mention of the reciprocality of genuine niceness does not seem to find its way into the reams of written work on doing business.

How bizarre.

In my pursuit of freedom through information I have studied everything from religion to spirituality, from theology to philosophy and law, and of course I have read – looking for inspiration – plenty about business; the art of making a living. I have read books by the guys and gals that have made it, lost it, lost it and made it back again, made it and given it all away, made it and squandered it, and even those that made it and hid the proceeds under the bed in a biscuit tin for fear of losing it all. The books have all been enlightening. Even the ones that were terrible taught me about where I didn't want to be. Many of the books talked about the win-win mentality, about ethics, about morals, about profit and loss, courage in business, risk taking, innovation, speculation, and dedication. Some quoted great sages, philosophers and gurus and taught about the dangers of money and power. But none advised me about the most important lesson in business: Be nice. Simply be nice. It is not hard. It costs nothing and it goes a hell of a long way (and comes back laden with profit).

The business world can often be a very difficult, cynical environment. People are often guilty of believing that everyone has an agenda – especially those who dare to be nice, those that dare to give and ask nothing in return. Those who scratch backs without asking for their own to be scratched are often judged with the utmost scepticism. Nobody does anything for nothing. There is no such thing as a free lunch.

But of course this is not true. The best, most attractive, most inspiring people in my world are all nice. They all do things for me – and for many others – with no thought of profit. They are all generous. They are all kind and do good deeds purely for the love of doing them.

What you give out always returns. Always. It is the law.

I have a friend, Paul Abbot, who is an incredibly successful writer. For those who don't know him, he is probably the top British TV writer of all time. He is responsible for (most recently) *Shameless*, *Clocking Off*, *State of Play*, *Touching Evil* and *Linda Green* to name just a few of the shows he's created. He is also an extremely generous man, both with his time and his advice. He has deals and contracts and commissions coming out of his very eyes. People are throwing work at him. His work is amazing; his work ethic even more so. You might think that his success is simply because of his hard work. You'd be wrong. If you go to his house and watch how he works you will see why he is so successful. He never stops being nice. He never stops giving. His house is like Euston Station on a Friday afternoon with all the comings and goings of the people he is helping. He is a dynamo. His capacity to help others to fulfil their own ambitions and dreams seems limitless. He gets in loads and loads of work and gives much of it away to new writers, struggling writers, often writers that the system has chewed up and spat out. And the more he gives away the more he seems to get back.

Similarly, I am always hearing stories about how nice my friend Glenn Smith is, and how many people he helps without asking anything in return. And my Auntie May (sadly now deceased) literally filled the room with her capacity to be nice and to give for no other profit than the joy it brought her. The great thing about Paul and Glenn and May is that most of the people they look after are not even in a position to return the favour, or offer them anything other than gratitude. And yet the more they give the more they seem to get. The effect is amazing. Glenn is thriving in business and life, as is Paul, and although my Auntie May is no longer on this plane, she has found immortality in the minds of many people (not least mine) just because she was so generous and nice.

Ultimately, I have found that people want to work with people who are nice. Even if – at this present moment in time – their game is not as sharp as it might be. If they are nice, people will help them tighten their game, people will go out of their way to find, even create work for them. People will bend themselves into all sorts of contorted shapes (including over backwards) so that they can help. And I am not talking about pseudo-nice, nice for the effect, nice to fit in or even nice to impress. If the nice you are offering is not of the genuine variety then it is a lie. Dishonesty in business is always the eventual harbinger of doom. I am only talking about the genuine article. Being nice because it helps others.

There is no profit in being nice, unless being nice is congruent with who you actually are. I am sure that to some of the hard-line business people out there this might sound a little trite: 'Be a nice person. People like it when you are nice.' I have even been told that there is no room in business for nice people. (Business types often mistake nice for weak.) But I would argue that if you are not nice, there will ultimately be no room in business for you.

The meek (as they say) will inherit the earth, and whilst profit may sojourn with those who do not heed the rules, it will only find permanent abode with those who do.

Chapter 2

Carp Fishing

I can remember (as though it were yesterday) a troubling internal conflict that I was wrestling with about five-years ago. I was teaching in the beautiful city of Edinburgh, Scotland with my friend Peter Consterdine. But teaching was just one of the myriad balls I was juggling at the time. I was also right in the middle of a very big book signing tour (for *Watch My Back*) that saw me visiting 60 shops in about 32 cities, of which Edinburgh was but one. As well as the tour, the teaching, and the heavy travelling schedule, I had also undertaken a huge financial risk when I decided to amalgamate all my bouncer books (*Watch My Back*, *Bouncer* and *On The Door*) into a hardcover omnibus edition and self-publish it in a bid to make *The Sunday Times* bestseller list. As you can imagine

I was stretched. But I was handling it OK, that is, until fate intervened. Someone – disgruntled by my work, my success, my profile, by me – decided to make it their life's mission to slander and threaten me via the Letters page of the very magazine I was a columnist in. Now you might think that this is par for the course when you are a profiled author, but with everything I was already carrying this one thing seemed to tip me over the edge. I was becoming anxious and angry. The nature of the letters – very personal and derogatory – were both unjustified and unfair, but they nevertheless found page space and were read by thousands. The publication of these letters actually made me question whether I really wanted to write for this magazine anymore. It made me question whether I wanted the profile I was receiving and, in fact, whether I wanted to actually be on the martial-arts scene at all if it spawned and seemingly encouraged such inane negativity. At any other time I probably would have left the slander where it belonged – in the bin. But with my mind stretched and vulnerable it found its way through my bullshit detector and was stabbing at my sensitive underbelly. I was troubled so I spoke with Peter about it one night in the bar of the Malmaison Hotel.

Peter has always been a mentor to me. In fact, he was the one who initially took me under his wing and helped me develop some very raw ideas into books, tapes and seminars. He is largely responsible for the success I enjoy in the martial arts today. Peter listened intently, nodded wisely (as he does) and said, 'Geoff, it's carp fishing!'

I said (more than a little confused), 'Carp fishing?'

Peter explained.

He told me that he was watching television one day and happened to catch a news story about a professional angler who appeared on TV regularly and had won a lot of major championships. He'd been riding the high-tide of success when something happened that changed, nay ruined, his life.

Just before one of the major championships, he was accused of using illegal bait. Now Peter didn't say whether our man was guilty or innocent, but what he did say was that the guy became so worried/angry/incensed and stressed about the accusation that he became depressed, started taking medication, split up with his wife and even lost his home. Peter told me how he'd watched the story unfold on television and, dumfounded, thought to himself, 'It's just carp fishing. It's not cancer, it's not war in the Middle East, it's not starving children in Africa. It's carp fishing.' This guy had become so engrossed in his sport that, what had started out as a gentle pastime, had actually become his whole world, it had become everything. It was more important to him than his wife, his family, his home. Apparently it had become more important that his health and his sanity.

What Peter pointed out to me, and what has stayed with me ever since, is the fact that the criticism I was receiving, far from being important, was just carp fishing. It was an opinion. And an opinion from some yokel who had never stepped into the arena himself, someone who was probably very angry because I was out there doing it, an individual, while he was one of the faceless multitude that liked to jeer from the bleachers because they were too scared to step into the ring. As Peter said to me, 'It's one man, Geoff, and a few letters. It's not life and death.'

This reminded me of another friend who went to see his father – a war veteran – for advise about a problem he was having. His father asked him, 'Is someone going to kill you?' My friend said no. His father said, 'Then you don't really have a problem.'

What I learned from this valuable lesson is that we often take ourselves and our problems way too seriously. We focus on them so intently that we lose our valuable sense of perspective, and when this happens molehills quickly start becoming mountains, and as we should all know, mountains can often be (or appear to be) insurmountable.

I suppose what I am trying to say is that it's all about perspective, about not letting things become bigger than they really are. It is very difficult for the eyes to see clearly what the mind has got completely out of focus.

Chapter 3

Catching Crabs

I watched a documentary when I was younger about how fishermen catch crabs (no, not them kind). I watched in awe as these leathery-faced, salty men of the sea lowered a mesh basket onto the ocean bed and, in no time at all, caught a couple of unlikely crabs that crawled in via a small hole in the lid and made their first (inadvertent) steps from basket to crabstick. What fascinated me most was not that they had crawled into what seemed an obvious trap; rather I was disturbed by the fact that they did not crawl back out again, even when the fishermen removed the lid. Eventually the basket filled to the brim with crustaceans, yet still they didn't try to escape.

After a few minutes it became clear to me why.

Every time a crab tried to crawl out of the trap, the other crabs (the blighters) pulled him back in again. I was amazed! I was watching my life's metaphor. Every time I had ever tried to leave a bad job and break away, my peers, like the crabs, had pulled me back again. 'What do you want to leave for?' they would ask patronisingly. 'This is a steady job. It's safe.' Then came the *coup de grâce*: 'There's no security out there, you know!'

'But I hate it here,' I'd whine.

'You haven't given it a chance! You've only been here five minutes,' came the usual response. (In fact, I'd been there six years.)

'So how long have *you* been here then?' I asked one day, tired of the unchanging replies. The old guy, face like a walnut, thought for a second. 'Oh about thirty years.'

'And what do you think of it?'

'It's crap,' he said without hesitation. 'I hate the place.'

Similarly, when I told my (ex) wife that I wanted to leave my steady job at the chemical factory, her face turned rolled-in-flour white. The old crab, claws raised, on the offensive, went straight to work.

'But what will we do? What if we don't make the mortgage? What if it doesn't work out? What if... '

It usually only took a few 'what if's' to get my blood boiling.

As I watched the documentary, I noticed that, after being pulled back a few times, the disheartened crabs not only stopped trying to escape but they also joined the other crabs in pulling back those that did try.

I'd been pulled back so many times in my life that I too felt disheartened. Self-depreciation became part of my inner core. The moment an entrepreneurial thought entered my mind, it was drowned by the voices of my inner crabs. Many times I picked up my biro in a fit of inspiration to write my way out of the factory by penning (what I dreamed would be) the next bestseller, only to be thwarted by a faulty internal dialogue that was stronger than my will to continue. So the pen would be discarded and replaced by bicycle clips and a ride to the factory for a night shift that I abhorred.

Even today, 20-years on, the very thought of that long ride still inspires a depression that reminds me how grateful I am to have found a way out. I used to sit in the works canteen in the dead of night when everyone else was tucked up in bed and think, 'What can I do to get out of this nightmare?' I felt so trapped. I had a family, a mortgage, HP payments, three children, a cat and a Raleigh Racer; so many things that kept me glued to a job I hated. And the longer I stayed the more glue I got stuck in. I could never think of anything else I wanted to do other than write, but I had allowed others to convince me that

I was dreaming and that this was not a real option. I resigned myself to a nine-to-five, Monday-to-Friday life of oil and grime.

But, I convinced myself, it wasn't my fault. I was stuck in the factory because my wife wouldn't let me leave.

Then one night, after my usual session of Sunday-evening bitching, my wife did something unprecedented. She retracted her claws, told me to shut my moaning gob and get a job that I did like if I was so unhappy. She gave me her permission. Well, I nearly fell over with the shock.

That was when the realisation hit me like a hefty tax bill. She wasn't holding me back at all. My nightmarish employment was no more her fault than it was the fault of the old timers at the factory or my peers. The fault was entirely mine. I was up to my kneecaps in the brown stuff out of choice. Blaming others was my way of hiding from my own fear. Those around me only stopped me from climbing out of the basket because I let them. I realised at this point – looking in the mirror not at a hard-done-by 20-something but at a frightened youth – that if I didn't want to stay in a job, if I really wanted to leave the factory, leave the city, even leave the country for that matter, nothing and no one would be able to stop me. If I put my heart and soul into doing something, believed it could be done and had a little faith in my own power, even mountains would crumble.

I could do anything, I could be anything. This was my world, my incarnation. I snatched back my free will.

Shortly after the shock of this realisation, I left my steady job of seven years and entered the real world of opportunity and excitement. I have never looked back. It was brilliant, exciting and scary. So much to do, so many places to go. I made a decision; I climbed out of the basket.

A few years later my mates were all made redundant from the secure 'job-for-life' in the factory. Me, I realised that the only security I needed was the knowledge that no matter what happened, I could and would handle it.

Chapter 4

Change Chaser

Have you ever heard the saying (and thought, 'What the hell does that mean?'): 'Be careful what you wish for because you might just get it.' I heard this saying many years ago and sort of innately knew what it meant, even if, at the time, I could neither articulate it nor act upon it.

To me, it meant that you should be careful when practising manifestation (the art of manifesting your desires and intentions) because it is an awesomely potent force that works. You will get what you steadfastly wish for, but getting what you want comes with a price tag. That price tag is change.

I have been thinking a lot of late about why people don't succeed in life, and why so many settle for second best when the whole world is open to them. I realised that the main reason for failure is not fear of failure but rather fear of success. I have witnessed so many people stand at the doorway to greatness only to balk and pull back at the last minute because, on looking through, they realised that success was not just a change of job title or an award or more zeroes in the bank, rather success was and is (often) a complete change of identity, a complete change of who you are. This change can cause temporary, even permanent disorientation.

Change is a word often bandied about with a flippancy that does not convey its potential for danger.

Only very few people in society really get this. Fewer still have the bottle to take on this danger, go out and, rather than run from the change, face it and chase it.

Change chasers are the leaders of this world.

Change is the one thing that we as a species tend to fear the most. Why do we fear this seemingly insignificant word? Because 'change' translated means death. Death of the old, the out-worn, the worn-out and the redundant. Gandhi had a radical suggestion regarding change. He said that we should, 'Be the change we want to see.'

In other words, we should not just sit and wait for the clammy grip of inevitability, we should not cower in a hole hoping that somehow change might pass us by on its perpetual sweep of the universe. It suggests that we should put in our gum shields, bang on our bag gloves, get into the fray and out of the spectator stands, take on the odds and challenge change to take its best shot. We should anticipate change and be on its crest as the great wave comes in, ride it and use its latent and innate power to drive us.

If you be the change you want to see you take away its sting, you de-fang it. If you can be the change, if you are the change, if you live the change, how can you fear the change? How can you fear what you are?

It is not change that hurts, only our resistance to it.

The good news is that whilst change might mean death, it just as certainly means birth. You can't have one without the other. They are the opposite sides of the same coin. Death of the old, birth of the new. When the caterpillar emerges from its chrysalis, we see the birth of the butterfly. It has to die to the old before it can be born to the new. Change is going to happen anyway whether you like it or not. It is the only constant. So you have a choice; to cower and hide from the inevitable or to be brave and *be* the inevitable.

There is as much freedom in acceptance of change as there is pain in resisting change. But our free will, God's great gift to mankind, offers us a choice, an exciting and empowering third option; to garner our courage and *be* the constant, *be* the change.

Have a look at your life right now. What changes are you hiding from? Which fears are pinning you down? What would you really love to do but at the same time fear to do?

Why not empower yourself today and turn the tables on change by stepping out to meet it? You might be surprised to find a brand-new shiny you just waiting to shapeshift and emerge.

Chapter 5

Easy

Amongst other things, I write films for a living. It's easy. It must be because it is all I hear people say these days. 'Geoff doesn't do a real job,' they say, 'he writes all day. Writing is easy.'

Really?

Writing is my passion. I love it. It is what I do. But easy? I don't think so. Perhaps it seems easy from the sidelines but then everything is easy from the spectator's stand. Perhaps for the ignorant and the inexperienced it seems easy, but then everything is easy in hypothesis. I have found that those who have yet to live up to their own standards will employ any available excuse to keep their pen and paper in different rooms rather than write the blockbuster they keep threatening to produce.

When I was ignorant and inexperienced I did and said exactly the same.

Let me give you an example of how easy my job is. This is important. If people keep thinking that success (in any field) is easy, they will be ill-prepared when reality smacks them between the eyes with demands for a steel fixer's work ethic, a saint's patience and the tenacity of a Titan.

My first film went into production in January 2007. People said, 'It happened so quickly. Overnight!'

So far I have been on this film for 12 years.

I have lost count of the amount of drafts I've written. Some of the early critique bordered on abusive. Every major film company in Britain turned it down several times. (One of my films has been turned down by 75 different financers. In this industry that is not unusual.)

When I wrote my book *Watch My Back* it was a similar story. Everyone said, 'Who wants to read a book about a Coventry bouncer? Leave your number in the bin.' It was turned down by more companies than I care to remember. If Sharon hadn't insisted I keep trying, I fear I might have taken the advice that I kept getting and thrown it in the bin. It hurt, of course, and the only way I stayed afloat was to use that criticism to give me drive. (I'll fucking show you.) It was that attitude that helped me get the book onto *The Sunday Times* bestseller list. It helped me write a stage play that had a national tour. It helped me write a short film that attracted international film stars, a BAFTA and entry into over thirty international festivals.

The film that won the BAFTA, *Brown Paper Bag* did not attract any financing at all. No one wanted to make it. It was too bleak, too harsh, had been done before. No one thought it was good enough to finance, so we (the producer, Natasha Carlish, who re-mortgaged her house for the film, and I) financed it ourselves. The many rebuttals tempered and energised me. Then I wrote a feature film and raised (with Martin Carr, the producer and Neil Thompson, the director) over two million pounds in finance. It is difficult when you feel that you are not getting any encouragement, of course, but... I liked it. I loved it. I developed an iron resolve. It weathered me like an old oak. All the rebuttals, knock-backs and criticism have helped me to develop a sinewy self-belief and a self-reliance that is so muscular it has its own respiratory system.

I could go on but I think the point it clear. No one has it easy. Life is difficult. But difficult is a necessary pre-requisite to success.

Chapter 6

Everest

A friend wrote to me. He was in bits. He'd applied for money from a local screen agency to produce a film he had written and they had returned his script with a rebuttal and a list of notes on how unprepared they thought he and his work were. The critique (he felt) was so scathing that it made his eyes water. I knew the feeling.

I have been there so often that I've actually developed bark over my exterior to help weather the critical storms. My friend had taken the critique (or the 'beasting,' as he saw it) all rather personally and was struggling to carry on. He told me that he was going to give up writing because the film world was (in his words) 'biased, behind the times, judgmental and a bastard to boot.'

This knock-back, one of many I presume (in this very subjective and very demanding business, rebuttal comes with the everyday post), had all but floored him. He felt his work was ready, in shape and filmable, but when the experienced industry folks advised him that it wasn't (not yet), he chose to see it as personal insult rather than qualified critique.

I tried to advise him that what he was experiencing was film-making (certainly it was a big part of the process) and that he should get used to it, because it is unlikely to get easier as you climb higher. It can be soul destroying, sometimes it's boot-in-the-bollocks painful, but you can't by-pass it.

With a slight change in perception, chunks of hardship can be moulded into the building blocks of strong character. Adversity and advance are synonymous and, after all, it was the north wind that made the Vikings.

My friend was attempting to ascend the Everest that is making a movie but struggling (and bitching about – please don't bitch about) the altitude. It is tough at the high end of any business, not least film-making, where millions are lost on bad films, and bad films seem to be more the norm than the exception. His email reminded me of a documentary I'd watched on TV and I told him about it in the hopes that it might inspire him to carry on, despite his set-back.

The film was about a super-fit man who wanted to climb Everest. To make his dream a reality, he trained his body to perfection until he was all sinew and muscle. He thought that this would be enough. It wasn't until he actually found himself on the mountain, at base camp, that he realised his stamina fell short of the mark. His training was good, meticulous even; he could run a fast marathon, lift heavy weights and captain his body and mind through the most excruciating physical workouts.

What he hadn't prepared for (what you can't really prepare for) was the actuality of being (as the Everest stalwarts are fond of saying) 'on the mountain.' Because on the mountain the air is thin. Even helicopters fall out of the sky in these higher altitudes because the spinning blades can't find purchase. The lack of air makes breathing – even for the fittest athletes – difficult. And the higher you go (as in life) the thinner the air gets. This is why on the higher echelons of Everest (and of life) there are very few people.

Now, although this man had been told many times in his preparations that the air on Everest was thin and that it would make progress slow and breathing difficult, he never really heeded the council. Until, that is, on day one when his chest was as tight as a fat kid's school shirt and he couldn't catch his breath.

He complained to his companions, all experienced climbers, that he couldn't breathe properly and they duly advised him (and reminded him) that, when you are on the mountain, this is the norm.

'No,' he insisted, 'you don't understand. I'm a fit man. I am conditioned. I should be able to breathe easier.'

Patiently the message was reiterated. 'There is very little air on the mountain. The higher you go the less there is. The inability to be able to get your lungs full is normal.' Again, he complained. He was fit. Not being able to breathe was not normal for him.

As much as his companions tried to reassure him that the way he was feeling 'was normal' (one climber said, 'Look, if you wake up in the morning feeling shit when you're on the mountain, it's a good day'), the neophyte climber would not have any of it.

He was convinced that his breathlessness was an early sign of some mysterious mountain illness. He bitched so much that in the end one of the climbers pulled him to one side and said (very firmly), 'Listen! We're on Everest. It's a high mountain. There is no air. If you want more air climb a smaller fucking mountain.'

And here endeth the lesson.

I need to hear it sometimes. I need to be told every now and then to 'stop the bitching and get on with it.' I am always trying to reach higher peaks and often find myself ready throw in the towel, complaining about the discomfort, the lack of help, the inadequate industry support. Then I remind myself of this story. It always gets me psyched up, back on my feet and moving. I don't know about you but I don't want to climb small mountains. I want to ascend into the clouds with the legends. And if that means less air (I haven't got much 'air anyway), then so be it.

Chapter 7

Everything that Happens to Me is Good

I heard it the other day and it made me smile, so much so that I went and made myself a cup of tea.

Someone said (with a hint of a scorn and a peppering of self-pity), 'That Geoff Thompson bloke, he lives a charmed life. He has had it so easy.'

Another friend, a fellow writer, tilted a similar lance in my direction. He told me that his lack of commercial success was due to the fact that he has had so many things block his path (poor health, family issues, etc.) I, on the other hand, had succeeded only because I'd had it so easy. He said this like nothing bad has ever happened to me; as though I was somehow impervious to the slings and arrows of life.

I have to come clean though. He was right. They were all right. I do live a charmed life and I have had it easy; not because nothing bad has ever happened to me, rather because everything that has happened to me has been good.

Let me try and explain.

My lovely dad died recently.

It was good.

It was his time and I was pleased that he finally got to graduate from this hard university we call life. It broke my heart to see him suffering so much whilst he was ill. I couldn't even talk on the phone without breaking down. He had cancer. It found its way into his bones. Then he died. My dad lived a good life. He was a good man. He was loved by many, disliked by none. But he has finished his brief sojourn on this spinning globe and now he is home. And that is not just good, it is cause for celebration. He has left me with a great legacy of love and very valuable lessons; how to live bravely, how to die with dignity.

One of my gorgeous babies took an overdose of pain killers when she was 18 years old. I got the five a.m. phone call and my heavy heart bled. A five-minute journey to the hospital took a lifetime and when I arrived all the doctors could tell me was, 'We won't know until tomorrow.'

It was a long day. It was an even longer night.

Someone said, 'Terrible what's happened to your daughter.' I said, 'What's happened to my daughter is the best thing that could have happened.'

My girl had fallen into a dark and loveless chasm where even the voices of her kin could not be heard. She was in a relationship that was imprisoning and dangerously destructive and none of us – not me, not her sisters, not her mum – could break her out. When she lay in that hospital bed, a small voice (somewhere in my consciousness) said to me, 'We are sorry she is here but this is the only way we could get her out.'

I trusted that this was true and it was.

She recovered, she went to university and met a nice guy who was appreciative of her beauty and sensitive nature. She is now happy and training to be a teacher. What happened to my daughter saddened me beyond words, but what happened to my daughter was good.

My brother died violently. He was bloated and yellow and ravaged and… so very beautiful. I have never felt such profound love for anyone as I felt for Ray during his five fast days of slow dying. I loved his very bones. But my brother loved the drink and the drink loved my brother, so much so that the love affair killed him. There was more to it than that, of course. Drink was his armoury and life was his enemy and, well, you can guess the rest. When he died, it was not me he called out for. It was not my mother's name that bounced and echoed off the hospital walls, nor my dad's, nor the names of any of his four heartbroken children. He cried out the name of his drinking companion, another alcoholic that shared his oblivious and sad existence. It was difficult. But it was good. The friend that passed the bottle in long days of hard drinking was very human and very broken and he loved my brother. For that reason alone, I loved him. I was with Ray as his decaying body buckled and bled and closed down. It was one of the most harrowing experiences of my life. It was also one of the most beautiful experiences of my life. I felt privileged that he chose me to watch his back as he left this life for the next. What happened to my beautiful brother has informed everything I do, everything I write about and everything I think. The lessons he taught me – both good and bad – I pass on. They will (they have and will again) save others.

My brother's death was good.

I have another family member who is dangerously ill. The illness is self-inflicted. My close family and I are forced to stand by and watch this slow decline because we can't save someone who will not be saved. It is her life. It is her body. It is her soul. It is her story. What is happening obviously needs to happen. It is her journey and it is good because all journeys lead home. That is ultimately where we are all heading.

I also have my own story. Much of it does not make easy reading, especially my back-story. I carry the karma of the hundreds of guys that I fucked up on nightclub doors when I worked as a bouncer. It has been hard to forgive myself. No self-pity here. No regrets. It was all good. The pre-fight, in-fight and post-fight have all been excruciatingly good. I am left with the residual ache of remorse, lessons that are as profound as they are stark and reference points that add an empirical wisdom to every new situation that I bring upon myself. Re-living each teeth-smashing boot to the face, each concussive stamp and each spitting invective has been... uncomfortable. In my former incarnation as a man of lower consciousness, I also fucked around, lost my integrity, betrayed my ex-wife, stole, fenced stolen goods and hurt my kids with my thoughtless actions. You don't just do that shit and walk away without debt. The trail follows you until you find the courage to turn and face it and take the consequences. We all have to atone. My actions spawned ten years of karmic residue that have brought me sadness, self-hate, guilt, self-harm and illness. Each of these, however, represented a step on the ladder of consciousness that has delivered me to where I am now; a better, more beautiful place, physically, mentally and spiritually.

So it has all been good.

Very good.

The experiences that fell into the realms of excess have been especially good. The road of excess (as the poet William Blake said) leads to the palace of wisdom. Every excess I indulged produced a lesson so painful, so profound, so earth-moving that it permeated my whole consciousness.

Although I vow never to repeat these dark experiences, I know that life will continue to proffer some of its own. It does have a habit of providing the hammer, anvil and furnace to temper every blade. So, if in life's next instruction I find myself revisiting those shadowy places, I will do my very best to neither spin nor toil, neither will I complain because it will all be good.

Everything that happens to me is.

And when folks say, 'That Geoff Thompson bloke, he's got it so easy,' I will continue to smile. I will continue to drink my tea. Because I know they're right. I do.

Chapter 8

Forgiveness:
the Healthy Option

Have you ever noticed that when you mention things of a spiritual nature, eyes start to roll and conversational exits are surreptitiously sought? Is it, do you think, because the idea of seeking something unseen is completely at odds with today's body-obsessed culture? Myself, I've always had a deep interest in the spiritual. Though, I admit, during my woolly mammoth period as a bouncer it was buried beneath the fear of looking like a twat in front of my mates. Thus if spirituality came into the conversation I followed the norm and patronisingly 'eye-rolled' with the rest of the sheep. Now that I am a little more self-assured I don't need the kind of conditional security that the 'norm' offers. Instead I look to developing a deep-rooted internal security that is as steadfast as it is empowering. Where I once toiled for shallow, surface mastery – hitting hard, lifting heavy weights, looking good, building muscle – I now labour from the inside out, pumping 'cerebral iron' to build a deep, sinewy mentality. One of the hardest lessons I learned en route was the capacity to forgive.

They say that forgiveness is good for the soul. It is the doctrinal mainstay of just about every religious icon – from the Nazarene right through to Mahatma Gandhi – who has ever walked the earth. And yet when we examine the world in which we live, when we closely examine our own lives, we see that there are many people preaching forgiveness, but very few actually putting it into practise.

We claim to love those close to us yet we can't forgive our brother for a ten-year-old error in judgement, or our sister for some wrong she inflicted upon us last year. We can't forgive the foreman for the way he treats us on the factory floor, nor our neighbour for a minor misdemeanour. And we definitely can't exonerate ex-lovers for using us as a spousal punch-bag. It appears that we can't even forgive ourselves for stupid mistakes made on our own journey through life.

Oh, sometimes we feign forgiveness with the anaemic proclamation, 'I'll forgive you, but I'll never forget!' Or the equally unconvincing, 'I'll never completely forgive you!' But you can no sooner 'partially' forgive than you can 'partially' fall out of a tree. You either do or you do not.

We also have a great tendency to rationalise our blame with inane remarks like, 'Yea, but you don't know what she did to me. I can't forgive her.' We even seem perversely proud of ourselves when we don't forgive, as though it were a great virtue.

It is not virtuous. There is no great feat of strength in carrying the carcass of a long-dead argument. Holding a grudge is easy. You can do it without even trying.

To forgive! Now then, that's a horse of a different colour. It takes strength, discipline and great understanding in order to forgive. I believe it is a great weakness of the human spirit that forgiveness is not more widely practised.

Our lack of forgiveness is killing us – literally. Our failure to pardon manifests a resentment that grows with the passing of time. It becomes an internal time bomb of bitterness triggered and perpetuated by every unforgiving gesture. This has a catastrophic effect upon our physiology. Every time the grudge is replayed like an old movie in our mind's eye it activates the release of stress hormones into the blood stream, a physiological fight-or-flight. Your contentious thought is registered by the mid-brain as a physical threat, a saber-toothed tiger, if you like. But – and here's where the problems start – because the unforgiving thought is not physical threat but simply a reminiscence, behavioural fight-or-flight is not activated. We do not, therefore, run or fight for our lives so all those redundant stress hormones lay dormant in our bodies, acting like a toxic bath for the soft internal muscles like the heart, lungs, intestines, bladder and bowel. Even brain cells are killed by rogue stress hormones. Add to this the fact that your immune system is greatly impaired by the stress response and can't, under those circumstances, adequately defend the body against infiltrating viral and cancerous cells, and you have a recipe for disaster, even death.

It is already estimated that the majority of all contemporary illness finds its roots in stress.

So every time you relive past upsets (because you can't put them to bed with a heavy dose of forgiveness), your body actually relives them too, as though for the very first time. This means that someone who insulted you ten-years ago, who you haven't forgiven, is still insulting you today – and you're letting them!

Logically, the best way to stop people from hurting you is to forgive them. This is what author Charles Handy would call 'proper selfishness.' This exercise is not so much a means of helping others (though this too can be healthy) as it is a means of helping yourself.

Once you forgive a person you stop carrying them.

In my younger days, working as a nightclub bouncer, I held many grudges, and for several years. Every time I thought about my past tormentors I could literally feel the stress hormones going to work. I didn't realise that I was on a downwards spiral to ill-health. I am ashamed to admit that I was very proud of my collection of grudges and perennially laid them out on the table like favoured collectibles. I often bragged to others that, 'I will never forgive,' and 'one day I might even seek revenge.'

When I finally realised what I was doing to myself, or more specifically, what I was letting others do to me, I instantly let go of the past and forgave those who I had been carrying for so long. I felt as light as the proverbial feather. I also felt empowered. Now I always make a point of forgiving people when they upset my apple cart. I even try to forgive proactively before they even do anything to upset me.

Many people feel that forgiveness is a weakness and this discourages them from any active practise. In my experience, forgiveness is the shield and sword of the gods. It is a great strength that should be nurtured in all people.

Like most things in life it is better to start small and build up. Forgiveness needs to be localised. Forgive the small things and gradually build up to the big ones. Start with yourself. We all have skeletons in our closets. What ever they are, forgive yourself and move on.

As far as health and fitness is concerned, forgiveness is cathartic; an internal cleansing that is an integral piece of the longevity jigsaw. So if you want to stay fit for life, start with a little forgiveness.

Chapter 9

Goals

People often talk about success, about 'making it' and 'getting to the top.' Whilst goals are good and dreams are the stuff of life, neither is likely to transcend reverie without a little more detail and conviction. People want success but they don't know what in. They want to 'make it' but struggle to define the vital 'it' part of the equation. I admire those that aim for the top, however, I always find myself asking, 'To the top of what?' Ill-defined or vague goals need to be crystallised and put in print if they stand any chance at all of making it from fiction to fact.

In a famous survey carried out in 1953 at Yale University, each and every student was asked their views on a number of topics relating to the university; what they thought of the campus, the staff, the library, and the lecturers. Even their opinions on the campus canteen were sought. Every imaginable question about life at Yale (and in fact, life itself) was posed. One of the most intriguing questions asked of the final-year students was, 'Do you have goals?' This question was followed by, 'If you have goals, do you write them down?' Only ten per cent of those surveyed actually had goals and of these only a minute four per cent said they actually wrote their goals down.

Interesting, you'll probably agree; even disappointing. But not enough to write home to mum about. What was interesting, even disturbing, was the follow-up survey some twenty years later when Yale repeated the exercise. This time, rather than pose the same set of questions to the current crop of final-year students, they decided to throw a bit of currency at the project and find all the people from the original survey of 1953 to see if their youthful aspirations had come to fruition.

It was agreed, and after much globetrotting research the majority of those surveyed twenty years before were found and asked, 'How did your life turn out?'

Amazingly, the four per cent who had written down their goals were all hugely successful, in their health, their relationships, in their community and financial affairs. They were outstandingly different from everyone else surveyed. The four per cent were also financially independent. In fact, between them they were worth more than all the other 96 per cent – those who did not write down their goals – put together.

What this should tell you is that having life goals is not just important, it is fundamental. If you don't have them, you don't get them. And if you want them badly enough you'll make that extra commitment to write them down. It makes them official. You need a definite destination. How can you ever get there if you don't even know where 'there' is?

If you have ever read a motivational book you'll probably know this already. The word 'goal' is tumbling from the motivational lips of just about every success guru from Deepak Chopra to Anthony Robbins. And they are right. But what most sellers of success fail to mention is the fact that success (in whatever form you would like it) comes at a price. And I am not necessarily talking about money, but about time, risk, commitment and sacrifice. Goals cost and for those of us unable or unwilling to pay, fulfilment is rarely forthcoming. Rather than make these sacrifices and actively seek out their dreams, the majority sit waiting for success to come to them – and for free. They wait for providence and fortune to show them favour. But the millions seldom come to those who do not develop the millionaire mentality. Income and lifestyle rarely exceed personal development. So if you have a goal what you have to ask yourself is:

Am I prepared to pay the price and become the type of person it will take to get my goal?

I look at my friend Glenn, for instance. He is in fabulous physical shape. He has the kind of rippling torso that most men dream of seeing reflected back at them in the bathroom mirror; lots of sinewy muscle and no fat (don't you just hate that?) He's ripped like a skinless chicken. But of all the people that come to the gym looking to achieve a similar body, probably only five per cent ever end up looking like Glenn. Why? Because the 95 per cent are not prepared to become the type of person they need to be to get a beach physique. They don't want to pay the price. To get 'cut-up from the gut-up' you need to chart the right course, then have the discipline and the staying power to stick to it without deviating to the island of cake, or the port of beer-and-curry. To build a body like Glenn you have to make sacrifices and develop a powerful will that'll resist the Friday-night piss-up/Saturday-morning fry-up scenario that follows a working week at the computer. You need to set a course from where you are to where you would like to be. And to show your commitment that goal needs to be written down and deadlined (time limits can be extended or shortened, if necessary).

Diet – the ultimate discipline – is the pre-requisite of a good physique. You have to get your eating down to a fine art. But very few make it because the journey is too arduous. Some kid themselves that they can take out the bits they don't like (usually diet) and still make their destination. Certainly the early stages are difficult when you have to change a 25-year-old cake-and-cookie habit and replace it with a high-protein/low-fat regime.

Next on the course is the training. I know a million people that workout, but I only know one or two with anything like a good shape. Whenever I go to the gym I see people sweating their way around the free-weights and machines, making all the right noises. But a hard workout is not just about the sweat and strain. It's about the detail, working on the finer points and setting the right course.

Setting the right course

It is easy to say, 'Set a course to where you want to go and you'll get there.' People set courses all the time and still fail to reach their goal. This is usually because they inadvertently set the wrong course and end up at the wrong destination, or even worse, back where they started. You might be working extremely hard but are you working in the right direction?

I remember the time I wanted to develop a brilliant osoto-gari (a throwing technique in judo). I'd watched good judo players perform the move a thousand times. I'd seen detailed illustrations in books and even watched demonstrations of the throw on instructional videos. With my limited knowledge I set about achieving my goal. I practised hard and daily. I have always prided myself on being a tenacious – even obsessive – trainer. I practised osoto-gari thousands of times, to destruction in fact, but I was practising it wrong. Never mistake activity for progress. You could be the hardest worker in the world, but still fail because you are hacking away in the wrong jungle.

The destination was set, but my course was off; it only has to be slightly out for you to end up completely wrong. I became brilliant at doing osoto-gari the wrong way. Consequently, when I sparred with other players, I rarely pulled the throw off. Then I went to train with Neil Adams (Olympic silver medallist in judo). He knew the right way to do osoto-gari. He knew the right course. He looked at my technique and, in altering one or two minor points, he altered my entire course. And hey, presto, I got it. In fact, because I had been given the right map and wanted to get there badly enough, I reached my goal in record time.

So make sure that you set the right course and be prepared for the sacrifices that the journey demands. If you don't know the way, ask the right people, those who are already where you want to be.

The danger of goals

Goals are essential; we've established this much. And writing the goal down with an expected time of arrival is as pivotal as setting the right course. But as well as all the obvious risks of aiming high – the risk of failure, risk of success and risk of change – there is also a hidden risk: Goals can be dangerous. When we set goals, when we fully intend with all our heart to achieve them, we nearly always do. So what's the danger in that? The danger occurs when we don't set our goals high enough.

Sometimes we aim low and, guess what, we hit low. Small goals are fine when they act as stepping-stones to higher ideals, but they can be very unsatisfactory in themselves.

My friend Steve is a keen runner. The other day he went out for a jog. He set himself a goal of five miles. He was capable of more, 'But,' he always told me, 'I'm being realistic. I know I can do five. If I try for more, I might not make it.' Not the sort of mind-set that smashes records, I think you'll agree, but a common attitude nevertheless. He set five miles on his internal clock and his body fuelled him up for exactly that. By four-and-a-half miles he was flagging and every step was an effort. He made five miles but at the final furlong the lad was exhausted.

The next week, Dave, one of his friends at the running club, had to pull out of a ten-mile race. He asked Steve to take his place. Steve was unsure. He didn't think he could run ten miles; it was double his usual distance.

'Don't worry,' Dave said, 'just set your sights on ten. If you can't finish it's not the end of the world.' Steve ran the race, killed the ten miles and had a great time doing it. He injected necessity and the organism grew to compensate. He is now preparing for his first marathon.

If you set your sights too low your body and mind will fuel you accordingly. Setting achievable goals does not push and stretch our limits; implementing standards that are just beyond our reach does. Paradoxically, I would say, 'Don't set your sights so high on the first shot that you become overwhelmed.' Had Steve gone from a five-mile jog to the London marathon (26 miles) he might well have written a cheque that the bank could not honour.

So aim higher than you think you can manage, but not so high you lose sight of your goal.

Milo the Great

There is a wonderful story about Milo the Great, a historical strong man whose life goal was to carry a full-grown bull on his shoulders.

'Impossible,' said his friends.

'Oh yea?' he replied. 'Watch this space.'

Milo was strong both mentally and physically, but he knew he was not burly enough to carry a full-grown bull. So instead of making his way to the nearest farmer's field and trying to winch a horned beast onto his back, he went out and bought himself a calf and kept it in his back garden. Every day Milo would go out into the yard and – after a little warm-up – lift the calf onto his shoulders and walk around with it. Day by day, as the calf matured and fattened, Milo's strength grew to compensate. His legs expanded in width and strength and his torso transformed into the shape of a door wedge. Eventually, Milo – to the astonishment of all – could carry the full-grown bull on his shoulders. By picking up the bull as it grew, and subsequently pyramiding his own strength to match, he grew with the bull.

Your bull may not be a hairy creature with horns and a nose-ring (sounds like a girl I once dated), rather it might be your business, a college degree or a promotion at work. Perhaps your goal is to buy your dream house (with a bull-sized mortgage). It could be anything. Like Milo, you don't have to pick up the bull right away. It isn't always advisable to try. Instead, you should allow your growth to be gradual and organic.

For Milo, picking up the bull was done in pyramidic stages. He used short-term goals (picking up the calf every day) to power him towards his long-term ideal. You could use the same principle to buy your dream house, build your business or increase your fitness level. Many people have bought fabulous homes by using the calf/bull principle. They buy a small house, sell it and use the profit (plus their savings, perhaps) to move up the property ladder towards their dream cottage in the country. It can be done. Hard work? No harder than working your doo-daas off with no goal in mind.

I'm not saying that this is the only way. You can jump steps, climb up more than one rung at a time, but when you do the risk rises proportionately. It's all down to how much risk you can take. Some people crumble when danger comes aboard. Others thrive on it.

Goal pyramid

You could even build a goal pyramid to chart your steps from short-term to long-term goals. Mountaineers do this to allow themselves recuperation and acclimatisation to new heights. They make their way first to a base camp, acclimatise, then step by step, they scale to the summit of the mountain. When they get within reach of the top they rest, eat, acclimatise and then, when the weather is clement, they attempt the peak. It is all done in pyramidic steps. They set themselves daily goals, aiming to climb x amount of metres by nightfall. If conditions are favourable, they may (and often do) exceed their quota; on bad days they may not even leave the tent.

I remember my mum using this principle to help my dad lose weight. He was carrying a belt-busting belly that was getting unhealthy (and unsightly) but he wouldn't hear of going on a diet. His self-discipline wasn't up to the job. My mum, worried about his health, gradually started to cut the size of his dinner down a tiny bit at a time and over a long period. Before he knew it he was eating light and healthy meals and looking and feeling good. As the dinner sizes decreased, the weight fell off him. It was so gradual he hardly noticed.

The real value of setting goals is not, as you might imagine, in their achievement – arriving at our destination is secondary. The greatest benefit of setting and achieving goals is the skills, the discipline, the tenacity, the information and the leadership qualities you'll develop along the way. Your whole world will change immeasurably for the better as a consequence. The adversity of a hard climb is what forges character.

Follow the Yellow Brick Road

In the film *The Wizard of Oz*, Dorothy and her troupe of mates are seeking a common ideal – the Wizard, a man who (they believe) can help them to achieve their individual goals. Dorothy wants to get back home to Kansas, the Cowardly Lion wants to find courage, the Tin Man needs a heart and the Scarecrow is desperate for a brain. Each of them believes that the Wizard will simply give them, free of charge, their dream. But he doesn't. He can't. What he can and does do is give them the means to achieve their dreams. He sends them on a hunt and promises to help them when they return. After accidentally killing the Wicked Witch of the West ('I'm melting, I'm melting') they return to Oz. The Wizard reluctantly keeps his word. He gives the Cowardly Lion a medal of valour, the Tin Man a heart-shaped watch, the Scarecrow a university diploma and Dorothy the knowledge that the power to return home was in her all along. Whilst each believes they have been given their goal free of charge, in actuality they have, through their journey – first to Oz and then to kill the witch – earned it through their own efforts. On the journey, the Cowardly Lion develops courage by facing his fears and protecting his friends against the witch and her army of mad, flying monkeys. The Scarecrow develops his brain by working out intricate game plans to find and then escape the witch. The Tin Man develops a heart through a multitude of kind and charitable acts. What the Wizard gives them amounts to little more than trinkets, symbols of their courageous quest. Their real goal started to manifest when they committed themselves fully to the task and agreed to pay the toll and take the risks.

Goals are as individual as fingerprints and one man's nirvana is often another man's nervous breakdown. Whatever your goal, there is one thing I have learned and one thing I know: We can achieve anything, nothing is beyond us. If we set our goals to paper and intend them to happen, mountains will move and rivers will part.

When I look at my lofty, long-term objective from the safety of my king-sized duvet, I don't ask myself, 'Can I have this goal' because I already know I can. I can have anything, we all can. Rather I ask myself, 'Can I become the kind of person it will take to get it?' Who we become is far more important than what we get.

Chapter 10

Gratitude: a Bit of Invisible Support

Sometimes we get so caught up in the maelstrom of life, ambition and achievement that we fail to realise what is really important in our lives; our health and the love and health of those dear to us. We forget to stop and thank God for all that we have, all that we have had and all that we will receive in the future. I know that I am often guilty of this and it is something that I intend to remedy because gratitude is more vital to our well-being than money or position or prospects. It is only after we hit a snag in life – an illness, a loss, depression – that we stop to appreciate just what we have. It often seems that we don't really appreciate our lot until it might be taken away from us.

When I look at the people I admire – Jesus Christ, Deepak Chopra, Gandhi and Mother Teresa – I notice that they all start their day with meditation and prayer. A big part of their daily ritual consists of thanking God for everything they have. They start their day not by asking for more, but by giving thanks for what they have already received and for what they know they will receive in the future. Not only does this morning mediation give them the chance to offer gratitude, but it also gives them the opportunity to fuel-up – spiritually, mentally and physically – for the day. This is how great people achieve great things.

Mother Teresa said that without her morning prayer and meditation (like Deepak Chopra she started early in the day, from four until six a.m.), she could never have sustained herself throughout the day. The spiritually aware are not in the habit of relying entirely upon themselves to achieve great things. They rely on God and through Him all things are possible. We all need a bit of invisible support, even – perhaps especially – when we think we don't. Great people don't get themselves in a muddle (too often) and then run to prayer (like most of us) to get fixed up. They pray preventatively so that they don't end up in a muddle in the first place. One ounce of prevention, after all, is better than a pound of cure. It's a bit like filling your car with fuel in the morning in anticipation of the day's journey. It would be unwise to just get up and drive your vehicle until it runs out of fuel. If you are lucky you may end up broken down only yards away from a nearby garage (not too much of an inconvenience). You might, however, end up broken down miles from anywhere with a long and inconvenient walk to the nearest fuel station.

I don't know of anyone who has not reached a crisis point at least once in their lives and thought, 'I'll get myself right and then I'll change (and I mean it this time).' And then they get themselves right and they change, but the change only lasts long enough to get them out of the rough and then 'bang!', they (me, you, all of us) end up falling back into their old ways and the pain of the past is hardly remembered. What I am suggesting here – and this is as much for me as it is for you – is that the change you are always threatening (better diet, being more patient, less jealous) is far better implemented from the solid clearing of the healthy here-and-now than it is from the out-of-balance, destined-to-arrive tomorrow. It takes discipline, insight, courage and a heck of a lot of self-knowledge. But if you were to start now, while the idea is fresh in your mind, then before you know it you would be riding the next wave rather than being bashed against the rocks (again).

They say that pain is a good advisor, and it is. But – as the saying intimates – it involves pain. Now if we were able to employ honest perception ('I know what needs to be changed') and a bit of will ('I am strong enough to make that change'), we could avoid the worst pain by tackling it while it is still just a niggle on the periphery of our knowing.

Or you could simply wait (like the last time) to get yourself buried up to the neck in problems and then try and muster the courage to pull yourself back out again, likely with the promise that, 'I'll get myself right then I'll change (and I mean it this time').

Chapter 11

Have Your Cake and Eat It

Go into any bookshop worth its salt and you'll find a pile of books and magazines offering the latest lose-fat-and-still-eat-chips diet that will allow you – or your money back – to have your cake and eat it. Now I don't know about you, but as a man with the propensity to grow, after a two-week holiday in Florida, to the size of a small continent, I have tried all the fad diets. And they all work… but only for a while.

Almost as soon as you lose the pounds (sometimes stones) and your jeans stop straining at the seams, the very same weight – and a bit more (for inflation, I presume) – returns with a vengeance and you have to make new holes in your belt.

It's depressing, isn't it?

It wouldn't be so bad but all the really tasty stuff simply oozes fat-gut, weight gain. I only have to look at the biscuit barrel and I grow another chin. As little as a week on a take-away fest leaves me with a skin-coloured bum-bag that wobbles in time with my step. I can be good for months at a time, sometimes even longer, and my weight stays at a comfortable 13 stone nine. The minute I get a fry-up down my neck, though, my legs start going all Sumo.

When I was 19 and clothes-line thin I could empty the contents of an industrial fridge without clocking up a single extra number on the bathroom scales. In fact, I was so thin that I wanted to put on weight, but my in-a-hurry metabolism burnt calories as quickly as I could extract them from Kit-Kats and kormas.

Then I hit 30.

At thirty my internal calorie-crunching gizmo switched to a lazy three-day week. All of a sudden the nuts and crisps, the beers and curries started to take their toll and I developed what can only be described as a wide-load arse. My food-abuse period was over; the salad and chicken renaissance lay in wait.

From then on in my weight has gone up and down like a busy lift.

When the weight is off I float around like a feather-light thing in tight fitting tee shirts tucked into bottom-hugging jeans, nibbling on health biscuits that taste like manila envelopes. I take every opportunity to remove my top and bare my torso, even when the wind is whistling my nipples into biker studs.

When I'm thin, my self-esteem rises to the rooftops.

When the weight is on, however, a dark cloud descends on my day. My world becomes one of chip dinners (I hide away in greasy-Joe cafes), rationalisation, take-away curries, wine, and beer and puddings that I might as well mould right onto my belly. And the apparel changes accordingly; beltless trousers with the top two buttons undone, hidden by trench-coat sweatshirts that obliterate everything from the neck to the knees. Even sex takes a backseat because it involves nakedness and hours of holding in my belly. My self-esteem drags around behind me like a wedding train.

As I said, I have tried them all; high-protein diets that turn your stools to rocks (ouch), high-fibre diets that have you shitting through the eye of a needle, low-carb diets that leave you so hungry you start nicking food off the kids' plates and snacking on carpet tiles, food-combining diets that are so complicated your brain throbs like a hammered thumb and sends you racing to the nearest chippy for a carb/fat/calorie top-up. A man needs his strength after all.

And the fruit diet! What's that all about then? I've been on it and no matter how hard I've tried I can't make a grape look or taste like a Malteser!

So what is the answer? How do I keep my sylph-like physique with all the culinary temptations constantly battling to fatten me up?

After 40 years of counting calories, hunting for the fat content on the backs of crisp packets and watching my bungee-belly bounce backwards and forwards from six pack to party seven, I've come to the conclusion that disciplined light eating for the rest of my life is the only way to stop me from looking like a doughnut. It's difficult, and you can never let up, but it works. Have some of what you want, but not all of what you want; train every other day and you'll keep the fat-monster at bay.

I dream that the Hereafter might be a paradoxical universe where Mars Bars and crisp sandwiches are the vital sustenance of life. In the meantime, I'm going to heed my mum's advice (offered to me when I hit a hefty 16 stone): 'Walk past that chip shop, Geoffrey.'

Chapter 12

Intention

There has been much written of late about intention. Some say (and I agree with them) that intentions are the building blocks of the universe. What you strongly intend today you are sure to live out in all your tomorrows.

This is both exciting and terrifying.

Most of us are not well-practised with our intentions so we tend to create our universe accidentally, complete with cloud-bathing heavens and barrel-scraping hells. When we are in heaven we call it a fluke or a happy accident. When we are in hell we call it 'karmic return' or we talk about 'spiteful God.' The truth is neither. We are creators of denial, fashioning random realities with our unskilled and unschooled thoughts, then looking outside ourselves to praise or blame when our creation makes us happy or sends us into a dizzy depression.

People with a lower level of consciousness revel in the blame culture. It is not their fault that life is shit so they look for someone, anyone, to blame. This is a weak place to reside because it is so disempowering. There is no darker place than the one you're in when you're playing the blame game. The very act of blaming gives your power over to the object of your blame. If you blame God, then it means your situation will not change until God favours you. Similarly, if you blame the government, society, your country, city or town, if you blame your ex-wife or mate or teacher, then you give them the key to your cell and await their leniency.

You always become a prisoner of those you blame.

People with higher levels of consciousness always place themselves at cause. They blame no one. They understand that their reality is one of their own making and if they want to change it they have only to look to the man or woman in the mirror. This gives them the freedom to practise their intentions until they become expert enough to create something dazzling.

Those who blame do so because (deep down) they are afraid of responsibility. It is easier to hunt down a culpable scapegoat than it is to take the blame onto your own shoulders. Those that take responsibility do so because they are excited about the possibilities of creating a new and ever-improved reality.

Personally, before I accepted responsibility, I resided consecutively, sometimes concurrently, in both worlds.

In my time I have created health, wealth, happiness and material possessions with my very best intentions, whilst at the same time creating violence, illness, unhappiness and penury with my very worst. It was only when I took a hard and honest inventory of my life that I realised I was the creator of it all. I could trace every good and every bad result back to intentions – or strong and persistent thoughts – that I'd had. It was at this point that I got very scared. And it was at this point that I got very excited.

I was scared because although I realised I'd created this juxtaposition of realities, I wasn't exactly sure how. That made my reality very unpredictable. I was excited because I knew I could learn by using my own inadvertent experience as a reference point. I could learn from my own experience. And where the details were foggy I could borrow from the library of information that is currently available on the power of intention. I could become an expert and I could practise as much as I wanted.

And that is what I did.

So how do you practise intention?

First you have to accept that intention is a creative force. Not just your own intention, but the universal intention that you click into when you practise. If you don't at least have an intellectual understanding of your own power then you are doomed to spin in an ever increasing cycle of random creation where life will bring you joy one day and a punch in the eye the next.

Search out the truth from another source, if you desire. It is in the Bible, it is in the Bhagavad-gita, the Koran, and the Tao Te Ching. Buddhism's basic tenant is that we create our own universe. Even new science is catching up with theories of Quantum mechanics (see the film, *What The Bleep Do We Know* or look at Deepak Chopra's work on the science of intention).

Once you accept the premise the training can begin.

You practise intention the same way as you would practice anything that you want to become expert in; with study and diligence. To become a strong judo player I read everything on judo. I placed myself in front of world-class teachers, I talked judo, I watched judo, I actually lived and breathed judo. But more than anything else I practised judo. I drilled and drilled and drilled the techniques until I was expert, until I could close my eyes and feel them, until I was the techniques and could handle judo players on the international scene.

Intention is no different. If you are a weekend player, you will get weekend results. If you practise four or five times a week, you'll start to see some decent movement. If you make it your life, you will rise rapidly into the higher echelons.

You start by investing in the information and instruction. Buy the books (my book, *The Elephant and the Twig*; any of Deepak Chopra's works; *The Field: The Quest for the Secret Force of the Universe* by Lynne McTaggart), attend the seminars (if you don't invest in you who will?), then practise what you have learned and be the proof that it works. There is nothing like actual hands-on experience to cement a truth in place.

For me, intention is about everything I do. If I want to create good health then I intend good health by seeing it, hearing it, reading it, talking it and doing all the things that constitute good health. If it is wealth I am after, then I do the same thing. I dwell on wealth until I start to draw it, or the opportunities to make it, into my life. People that make themselves ill practice intention without realising it. They think illness, they see and fear illness, they talk it, read it, watch it and live it until eventually they manifest all the fine and grizzly details in their own bodies.

I have a friend of a friend who is a very successful woman. She is at the top of her field. It wasn't always that way. When she was younger and her mind was undisciplined she was always suffering with psychosomatic illnesses that would often lay her up for weeks, sometimes months at a time. She even convinced herself once that she had a brain tumour. She thought about it all day long. She read about tumours in her medical books and read articles about the symptoms in medical journals until, in a short time, she actually started to manifest these symptoms herself. She became so convinced she had a brain tumour that she went blind in her left eye. She was finally taken into the hospital for a brain scan. The scan was clear. There was nothing physically wrong with her. She had no tumour. Interestingly, as soon as she got the results, the sight in her left eye returned. Then she had a thought; if her mind was so powerful that it could manifest blindness, how much more could she manifest if she schooled and disciplined her thought and put her intention to work on good things?

People that create great wealth click into the same power. When the actor Jim Carey was going through a very difficult phase as a stand-up comedian he drove up to Mulholland Drive in the Hollywood hills and decided that he was no longer prepared to work for peanuts. He was no longer prepared to be an also-ran stand-up comedian dying on stage night after night in front of a partisan crowd. So he took his bank book out and wrote himself a cheque for $10 million. He vowed that he would be earning that amount per film within ten years.

He was wrong.

Ten years later he was an actor in Hollywood, but he wasn't earning $10 million. He was earning $20 million. His intention was so solid that he wrote it down and then never lost the faith until his dream was a reality.

You practise by doing, and doing involves thinking, seeing, hearing, feeling, smelling and intuiting your intention until your thoughts coagulate and become manifest. Whether you intend to paint the front room or climb Mount Everest, the process is the same.

Intention is a very learnable technique. If you can learn to drive then you can learn to intend. And if you intend enough, you can become an authority.

Why not try?

Chapter 13

Looking Out, Looking In

Another marathon, another black belt, another gruelling, physically-stretching, pain-inducing endeavour where we venture out bravely to our furthest limits. The elements are conquered. We get a pat on the back, a medal, a trophy, admiration from our peers and awards stacked up on our shelves. How brave, how exciting, how very fucking invigorating. We take a little rest then onto the next extreme challenge, the next unchartered landscape that we can not only attack but also tell our friends that we are going to attack so that they can flatter us with their admiration. The praise comes at us like a sickly sweet chocolate waterfall and we let it shower over us.

It's good to be brave.

But how brave are we?

Do we choose the fights that we know we can win (even though we tell ourselves how extremely dangerous they are?) Are we guilty of racing out there pretending to look for the unchartered when actually we know that all of it is chartered and – although certainly physically demanding – has been done before?

In order to be really brave, to be really extreme, to be really daring and adventurous and to really (I mean really) look death in the eye and take our hearts (and our arses) in our hands, we need never do another climb, race another marathon, face another black belt panel or fight another monster on the nightclub door. In fact, I'd say that if we really want to stop pretending, we don't need to leave the city that we live in, the town, the road, the street, the house, the room or even our own skin, ever again. If we really want to be brave we just need to close our eyes, stop going out and start going in.

Fuck Nanga Parbat, fuck the one-hundred-man kumite, fuck the marathon across the desert or the triathlon across broken glass in bare feet. Fuck all of that because it is old hat, it has all been done. That old parrot of a challenge is dead. It is all boringly predictable compared to the real challenge of going inside and taking a cold, hard, honest look at yourself – and then changing the bits that no longer serve. Actually, even before that it would be a start to admit the fact that the man or woman that you look at in the bathroom mirror every day is deeply flawed. The man or woman with ten black-belt certificates in ten different styles from ten different masters who the outside world thinks is granite tough is not even tough enough to leave the job they hate, the spouse who treats them badly, the city that no longer nourishes them and the habits that bleed them dry because they are frightened of real change. Real change is full of uncertainty.

The man who impressed the living shit out of everyone by climbing ten peaks in ten months and who lost ten toes to frostbite is not even strong enough to resist temptation. Instead, he loses his integrity by sleeping with his best mate's wife. For a five second spurty tingle of cloudy liquid, he loses his soul.

Most of us think we are tough but most of us are not even tough enough to deal with the greed and envy in our gut, the panic and fear in our chest, the repressed rage that is hooked and fish-boned into the flesh of our throats or the jealousy that rages in our heads. We feel tough but we can't control what we eat and what we drink and what we ingest. We feel strong yet we let our thoughts kick sand in our faces. We feel manly and yet we fear to cry. We claim power and yet we lack even the power to change.

So we go out, we do courses, we listen to lectures, we take yoga (five different styles), we lift weights, or go to step class or learn Qui Gung or Tai Chi. We read the Bible, we devour the I-Ching or memorise the Bhagavad-gita. When we feel spiritual we quote Lao Tzu and when we feel angry we fire invectives from Sun Tzu. We talk about the Upanishads ('What, you haven't read the Upanishads?'), we meditate, contemplate, whirl like a dervish, chant, have homeopathy, get our feet massaged, have our scalps fingered by a dark-skinned chip fryer from Bolton, do the tarot, have our runes read, visit spiritual healers, sun worship, go on a fucking retreat and talk to fucking trees.

We go out and we do it all. And that's the point. We are going out but we're not going in. Out there is the path that is so well-travelled that the ground is flat. There is only one path that is not only less travelled, but not fucking travelled at all. That is that one true path that leads us into the murky quarry, the slushy cerebral dumping ground where the decomposing (but still very alive) bodies of our pasts lie waiting not only for their reckoning, not only for their release date, not only for their say but for their redemption.

It is hard to look at what you did, what was done to you, how you were treated and how you treated others. It is hard to look the many versions of the old you in the eye and say, 'Actually, I don't like you. I don't like what you are, what you did. I don't like what you didn't do. I don't like what you became.

I don't like what you allowed yourself to become. I don't understand you.' That's difficult. That's a mountain to climb, that is a fearsome one-hundred-man kumite (each opponent a version of the old you with a grudge to bear and a bloody axe to grind), but it gets even harder. To ensure the release of these trapped entities you don't just have to acknowledge them and look them in the eye; you have to face them and say, 'I forgive you, I forgive them. I let me (all of me) go. I let them go.'

Do the marathon if it serves you. Climb the mountain if it is a workout you are looking for. But if you really want peace, stop working out and start working in.

Chapter 14

Night-travellers

I thought you might be interested in a conversation I had at the weekend with my writer friend, Paul Abbot. Most of us spend our days looking for comfort and avoiding discomfort. This means that we avoid fear at all costs. When I asked Paul what it was that most drew him to a new project, he said it was fear. The work that scared him most was the work he wanted to do. In fact, he said that if the work didn't scare the crap out of him, he didn't do it because fear was the key ingredient in making great television (or great anything). Ray Winstone said a similar thing to me when we were filming *Bouncer*. He said he liked doing the work that frightened him. The challenge to him and to Paul was not in just facing down the fear, but in using the fear as alchemistic base metal to make gold.

Most of us walk around thinking that we are the only people in the world who feel fear. Because of this we avoid things that frighten us, which means we stop growing. People like Paul and Ray are what the poet Rumi called 'night-travellers', people who go into the night and hunt down their fears. They do this because (as Rumi said) the moon shines on night-travellers. Light and knowledge are given to those brave enough to turn and face their fears. The people who see red lights as green, those who lean into the sharp edges are the very people that become ultra successful. It is not that these people do not feel fear. They feel it just the same, sometimes even more acutely than everyone else. It is only that they change their perception of fear. They learn to love the adrenalin and they turn that raw energy into success.

So, what it is that you are avoiding? What is it that you fear?

Maybe now is the time to be brave and turn into the dark, take a step towards it, creep up on it, break off its four corners or – if you are really courageous – dive into it head first and see what happens. You might be surprised to find that fear is not the enemy you always thought it to be. You may be even more surprised to find that buried within that fear is a golden nugget of information that can't be found anywhere else on this earth.

Start now. Be brazen. Be brave. Make the decision. And when the fear rears its ugly head, look it in the eye and dare it to do its worst. Then watch your three-dimensional demon turn into a two-dimensional cartoon and quickly disappear. Fear feeds on your terror. It is nourished by those who turn and run. Courage is the killer of weeds like fear. When you stand and endure, that molten metal of fear inside you turns to gold.

Be a night-traveller!

Chapter 15

Reciprocal Returns

The lad that was visiting my master class was young, maybe 22, and very fit. He knew his way around the mat as far as the ground work was concerned but he was getting tapped out again and again by a succession of my instructors. Not only was he getting tapped out, he was completely out of his depth. I could tell by his face (dispirited), his gait (shoulders hunched, defeated walk) and his eyes (they hit the ground like dropped marbles) that he'd expected a little more of himself. He knew (he later confided) that my class was tough and that the fighters were top drawer but he thought he might at least be able to hold his own.

After the session he asked me where he had gone wrong. To be frank, I wasn't sure. I watched him fight three or four times and all I could see was that he was out-gunned by better players than himself. I couldn't quite put my finger on why there was such a disparity between his ability and that of my people. I was confused so I decided to do a bit of probing.

'How often do you train?' I asked, hoping that his training routine might shed some light on the issue. 'Oh,' he replied (a little too keenly) 'I train twice a week. Without fail.' I remember thinking: Twice a week! Without fail!

I smiled, 'Well that's your problem.' I told him, 'You are training twice a week, these guys are training twice a day. By Monday night they've already done your week's quota of training.'

My visiting martial artist was making the same mistake as many. He was training recreationally and expecting professional results. This is a bit like planting cabbage in your garden and expecting roses in the summer. This problem does not just confine itself to the martial arts. I see the same attitude in all walks of life. Fair-weather golfers who get their clubs out every summer and then wonder why their handicap remains a handicap. Footballers who train on a Wednesday and play on a Sunday but dream of kicking a premiership ball in front of 50,000 screaming fans on a Saturday afternoon. Painters who imagine that three hours at the easel is going to turn them into the next David Hockney. The writing world (similarly) is full of part-time hacks that throw out a weekend script and then bitch because Hollywood does not recognise their genius.

This (I have found) is a universe that gives out what it gets in. The returns are entirely reciprocal. This is good news and bad. Good because it means that anyone who invests their time diligently can expect great returns; bad news because those that want to change what they are getting without changing what they are giving have a lot of stepping up to do.

I am amazed by the amount of people I see who are treading water, banging in the minimal investment and then sitting around waiting for the floodgates of great returns to open up for them. People want gain without pain, profit without investment and reward without risk. And when it doesn't materialise they look outside of themselves and blame.

The law of reciprocal returns is very exciting. It means that you can have anything if you are prepared to do the work and handle the pressure. And its mandate is very clear:

Step up, or shut up!

Chapter 16

Suffering

We are all suffering. There is a fair chance that you are suffering right now and are looking for balm, something – a word, an idea, a sentence, a premise, a medicine, maybe a chant – that might help ease your pain. As a man that has suffered a lot I am no different to anyone else. I want to understand the nature of my suffering and replace it with a heavy dose of peace. If I can't do this, if my suffering is unavoidable, then I at least want to make sense of it. I want my suffering to be for a reason. My sojourn on this globe is not a long one, maybe one century if I am blessed, so I don't really want to spend any of it suffering unless I can profit from the experience. We can all endure suffering if we know why. Nietzsche said that if we know the why we can endure almost anything.

In my bid for knowledge, I (like most) left my city, left my country, actually even left my body in search of the pain panacea. Outside, in books or conversations with gurus, I found no such relief (other than the temporary inspiration that good information affords). Instead I found direction in the guise of a finger that pointed not East, not to the temples of Tibet or the churches of Rome, but back to Coventry, back to my house, my garden, my body. Deeper still, it pointed back to that dark nothingness that pervades all things when I close my eyes.

Every time I go out I am directed back in. Every time I try to run I am encouraged to wait and see. Every time I hide I am advised to try visibility instead. Go inside. Have a good look at the discomfort that resides there. Why? Because suffering is the body's way of telling us that something is wrong. And if we keep covering the message with artificial blankets (painkillers, drink, drugs, sex, denial) we might never know what the suffering means. That never knowing could kill us, or worse still, it could lead us into a long life of unnecessary pain.

From my limited understanding, there are two kinds of suffering. The suffering that we inflict on ourselves, and the suffering that is inflicted up on us by circumstance.

The suffering that we bring on ourselves, we should (if at all possible) eradicate. There is no joy and little gain in suffering unnecessarily. To stop this kind of suffering, we need clinical self-honesty. Nearly all suffering can be traced back to the self. If you are really honest, if you own everything, if you place yourself at cause and expect nothing from anyone, and if you can stop your negative thoughts, most of your suffering will end.

No one can offend us, no one can let us down, no one can abandon us, disappoint us, make us jealous, cheat us, make us envious, angry, greedy, depressed, poor, under-educated, fat or unfit. These are all circumstances that we readily accept, perhaps because we do not know any better, perhaps because we are too lazy to change.

Do we enjoy being a martyr to our suffering?

At one time or another I have fallen into all of these categories. But I have since learned to recognise that I am the centre of my universe. The responsibility for my health, wealth and happiness lies not with the hospitals and doctors, not with the government and certainly not with other people. The moment we rely on outside forces for our well-being, we become their prisoners.

The responsibility lies with you.

If your suffering is health related, why not make it your life's mission to understand your body; find out how to get well and stay well. Become an expert, do a degree, an MA, a PHD; become the most knowledgable person on the planet with regards to your health.

If your suffering is economic, who do you think is going to change your situation if you don't? There is no one coming to your rescue. There are no more heroes. Study economics, put yourself into an apprenticeship with the wealthy and the rich. Study business and make yourself a man of great economic knowledge. The information is all out there, much of it free. Don't blame any outside forces. Don't blame the government because of the poor minimum wage. Don't blame the conglomerates for stealing too much of the pie. Blame is the predictable response of the masses and once employed it knows no end. So get out there, earn your worth and ease your suffering.

If your suffering is mental, make it your life's work to understand the cerebral schematic and put that information to work for you. In fact, make that information public so that you not only ease your own suffering, you ease the suffering of all those who find themselves in your situation. Scour the internet, invest in books, lectures and courses. Talk to the psychologically robust, ask them their secrets, then put that information into use and be the proof that it works.

These options are open to everyone. But information will not drop out of the sky. You need to hunt it down. It can be done. It has been done. History is brimming with folks that have taken responsibility for their own suffering and have not only succeeded in easing their pain, but have become massively successful at the same time.

Austrian neurologist Viktor Frankl said that all suffering is relative. Whether you are lying in bed sweating and manically depressed at three a.m., or you are a Holocaust survivor (like him), your suffering will feel as though it knows no depths. It has been proven by psychologists that the symptoms of manic depression can be as frightening to the sufferer as climbing out of a dug-out with a bayonet to engage in mortal combat.

What I have learned from my suffering is that I don't like it much. But if I can't get out of it immediately, I am going to learn as much from it as I can. Much of the greatest stuff I have learned in the last 46 years has come directly from periods of suffering. In fact, I would say that personal development is a natural by-product of enduring pain, that is, if you are wise enough to look inside rather than outside.

The Sufi poet Rumi said that the chickpea only got its flavour from being boiled in the pot. When it tried to jump out to escape its suffering, the cook pushed it back in with the ladle and said, 'You think I'm torturing you. I'm not. I am boiling you to make you sweet.'

When we are suffering, we all tend to look for an escape. If there is a way out, my recommendation is that you take it. But heed the advise on offer. Your suffering wants you to see something. Do not turn away. Address it. Right now if you can. If you don't, you will find yourself back in the middle of your suffering, again and again, until you get it. Once you are in possession of the vital information you need, leave your suffering behind. Take responsibility, make decisions, change and adapt. Do what is necessary, but leave it behind.

Sometimes you can't.

In these circumstances, Frankl suggests doing something radical. My experiences have led me to the same conclusion. You must be worthy of your suffering. Handle it. He said that there is great liberty in suffering, that we have the opportunity in our darkest moments to reach a higher consciousness through endurance. It is an opportunity offered to few people. This doesn't mean that you just accept suffering, but you endure it stoically while actively looking for a solution.

Pain is a great adviser. Suffering is wise counsel. If you are brave enough to look closely at them, they offer you great secrets. The answer is always hidden within the problem.

If you go into your pain, if you are brave enough to do that, to sit in it and examine it minutely, then the self-inflicted suffering will disappear (because it only feeds on fear). Your life-imposed suffering can offer you transcendence.

Suffering ceases to be suffering when we truly lose our fear of suffering. No one can help you with this. It's up to you. Once you take responsibility for yourself, you will draw assistance from every living corner of the universe.

Chapter 17

The Art of Restriction

When I first started working as a club doorman all those years ago, the thing that struck me most (scared the shit out of me actually) was how restrictive a real confrontation is when it comes to space. It didn't seem to matter whether you were fighting on four acres of mown grass or three-square-feet of pissy pub toilet, the fight always ended up very close and personal. There was rarely any room for manoeuvre.

This is why (and when) I started to experiment with very close range combat. I specialised in punching, because punching is the range most consistently available in a real fight and, culturally, pugilism suited me. I realised way back then that in a fight you very rarely had more than 18 inches of space to work in. Yet all around me there were martial artists practising in a range of three feet or more and using techniques that would not be possible in a live encounter. To try to mend this gaping hole in contemporary combat, for me and for anyone else interested in taking it to the concrete, I developed what I called 'restrictive training.'

By using this technique I was able to summon instant power from any position and at any range, even the most restrictive. Whether I was in a car or a phone booth, a toilet cubicle or a farmer's field, I was able to draw an explosion of power from (seemingly) nothing. I encouraged my students to punch from seated positions (floor, chair, etc.), kneeling positions; from on their backs, their bellies, with their backs against the wall – from anywhere that massively restricted their movements. From restricted positions you are unable to employ hip twist or use momentum to garner power. This restriction forces you to 'find' something else. And you do. Very quickly.

Because of restriction of movement and space, we started to develop massive relaxation through necessity. When you have no range of movement, tension and stiffness completely impede any power. We started to employ joints (the more the better) in the technique, so that (for instance) if I was in a phone booth or a toilet cubicle or on a packed dance floor, I could summon tremendous power and explosion without even moving my feet. And then there was intent, one of the first things that starts to grow when space is at a premium. You realise very quickly that intent of power is power. Then there is that certain something that only restriction training can develop, an indefinable energy, an explosion at the end of the technique that cannot be brought or bartered. You won't find it in a book or on a tape or even in a class. The Chinese call it 'chi,' the Japanese 'qui.' It has as many names as there are cultures. Personally I don't want to place a name to it or throw a shroud of mystique around it. I can't claim to know what the energy is other than an accident. Restrictive training helps you to become accident prone. It works so well that folks have to start pulling their punches because the power they are generating is too much for their bones (they start picking up injuries) and too much for the bones of their opponents. Not only does restrictive training force people to find some other source of power than the one that they normally employ, it also acts as an accelerator; people become big hitters much faster than normal. It would be no exaggeration to say that I get people punching twice as hard within one session using this method.

But being able to punch hard is not what excites me about restrictive training.

What I really love about it is the fact that it enables you to view life restrictions from a totally different and positive perspective. Just as restriction can trigger the release of chi in physical training so can restriction in life (if viewed correctly) enable you to discover a reservoir of hitherto untapped power.

Lance Armstrong was given a life-threatening restriction called cancer. He had a choice. Lie down and take it and probably die within a year, or find something that would not only enable him to heal, but also give him the power to win the Tour de France an unprecedented eight times. Do you know that he was so dominant in the Tour that the organisers changed the route several times to give the other riders a chance at winning?

I was bullied at school and suffered badly from depression. I had a choice. Accept this and live a life of mediocrity and fear, or find something inside me, some force, some power that would not only elevate me above my playground tormentors, but also take me to the world stage in martial arts and in writing.

Everyone reading this is restricted in one way or another. It might be a health issue or a relationship problem, it might be money or fear. Your restriction could be that you are without direction or hope. If you are like most people (I hope you are not), you are probably looking outside of yourself for someone to blame. If you have the courage to stop projecting and look inside youself you might be surprised to find that there is an infinite amount of power available to you within the very restriction you are trying to escape.

Many people (I count myself as one of them) go into life and search out restriction in order that they might grow. They seek out tough martial arts schools where they are at the bottom of the class, difficult jobs where they feel out of their depth, situations that scare them, places (inside and out) that expose their cracks. Some people are really brave and restrict themselves with the little things that make the biggest difference – things like diet, personal discipline, counselling, and psychotherapy. Others (and I also include myself in this group) have no need to go in search of restriction because restriction has been thrust upon them by illness, money or family problems. Either way, your route to the stars is not to turn your back on restriction and kick and scream and wish it gone, but rather it is to turn into it, grab your spade of courage and dig deep. Somewhere within the problem you are facing right now is the answer that you have been looking for your whole life.

Chapter 18

The Blame Trap

As a species we have the power to change the world (certainly our own world). Of this I have no doubt. In fact, I am the living embodiment of my 'live-it-now and do-it-all' philosophy. I live my life in the creation business. I create my world. I love every minute of it. Thus far I have managed to make manifest every desire I have set my intention on. This is not meant to sound smug. I see myself as a very ordinary person who has managed to liberate himself from a life of unnecessary toil. If I can do it, believe me, anyone can.

I measure my accomplishment not by the balance in my bank (though lots of noughts can be very pleasing), but by the fact that when I get up in the morning and when I go to bed at night, I feel happy. That's what makes me a success.

As a child I always dreamed of making my living as a writer. As an adult that is exactly what puts bread on my table from one day to the next. Success, of course, is very subjective. Your idea of nirvana may be – and very likely is – entirely different from mine. As long as what you do makes you happy then it would be fair to say you are a success. It's when you spend your life doing the things you don't like that the Monday morning feeling stretches through until Friday afternoon and Sundays are a dread because they precede Monday. That's when you find yourself thinking, 'Is this what I really want to do with my life?' This is especially true if you feel you have no other choice.

People are forever telling me that they would love to write, to sculpt, to garden, or to teach but they can't because their life, their wife, the mortgage, the kids, their environment, their circumstances – even God – won't allow it. This very statement, one I used (to death) as a younger man, is a self-fulfilling prophecy. It is probably the most over-used and certainly the most disempowering combination of words you could ever make the mistake of employing. It does exactly what it says on the tin. If you can't do what you want to do because you wife says so, you give her all your power. That means that until she says yes, you're stuck where you are. If you blame the environment, circumstance or your upbringing, you give all your power over to these inanimates. And, again, it means that, until they favour you, you're glued to mediocrity. If you believe you are powerless (the moment you fall into the blame trap you *are* powerless), then by definition you are exactly that.

The reason I know this is because I have fallen into the same trap more times than I care to remember. As a fledgling, I spent my days wallowing in procrastination, blame and self-pity. I hated my lot but, of course, my lot was never my fault (is it ever?)

The answer is as simple as a Greek drama. Take back the responsibility for your own creative power. Admit ownership of your future then set about building a palatial existence that makes you happy, and by extension, makes all those you love happy also. It takes bollocks of cast-iron to take the reins but if you want to trail-blaze then riding shotgun is not where it's at.

Think about the job you do for one moment. You probably spend two thirds (at least) of your waking life at work. Two-thirds! Now if you don't love the bones off your job, if you are not inspired to the point of exhilaration about the nuts and bolts of your current employment, if they don't have to drag you away from the office kicking and screaming at the end of each day because you want to do more, then you have to ask yourself, 'Why am I there?' Just hope that your first answer is not, 'The money!'

I am emphatic about this message so please don't think me conceited when I tell you that I love my life. I love being me. It wasn't always this way. I spent the first half of my life living other people's idea of normal. I hated it to pieces. Now I enjoy my life so much I don't want to sleep at night. I want to be out there experiencing everything.

You see, when you love what you do it stops being work and becomes fun. My working life is unconventional certainly, unpredictable definitely, and sometimes it scares the living shit out of me, for sure. But I like unconventional. I thrive on the unpredictability and (if I am being honest here), I like being scared. I love being overwhelmed, even out of my depth. I have become comfortable with discomfort because discomfort is a sign that I am growing. I don't want to be stuck in the middle of some cornflake-size comfort zone, sweeping around a metaphoric lathe. I want to be precariously balanced on some craggy precipice where I can see it all.

'Yea, I agree,' you might say, 'but (the obligatory BUT) it's really hard.'

Of course it's hard, it has to be hard. You can't temper a blade without putting it through a forge. What's the use of a blue ribbon when you haven't even run the race? It is difficult, but please, let's keep things in perspective here. Carrying a hod on a building site is back-breakingly hard, working your brain into mush on a computer everyday can be hard with a capital H. Any job, especially the ones you despise, that entails bargaining two-thirds of your life just to make the mortgage is harder than a big bag of hard things. We all know about hard. It's what we do on a daily basis. At least when your sweat is vocational, when you are hacking away in the right jungle, you can sit down at the end of another satisfying day and think, 'This is what I really want to do with my life.'

We are where we are in life through choice. (Oh yes we are, even if it is just the fact that we do not choose to change where we are.) If we don't like it, we have the God-given power to reinvent ourselves. The moment we think that we lack this power our thoughts make it so.

Someone dead famous (so famous I can't remember his name) once said (and he was right), 'If you think you can or you think you can't, you are right.'

Chapter 19

The Pornographic Wasp

If I told you that it was a wasp that taught me the dangers of pornography you'd probably accuse me of being a honeycomb short of the full hive, but it is true. Before I recount the lesson, I have a confession to make. I do like pornography.

Actually that is not entirely accurate.

Let's say that I am highly aroused by pornography.

I don't really like it because, well, like all addictions, it drains my energy. Sometimes it completely disempowers me. I am highly aroused by it because it is innate, it is my genes. So I don't watch it anymore. I don't read it. In fact, I don't entertain it at all. I haven't for many years. I let it go around about the same time that I stopped drinking alcohol. But I don't judge it either. I don't like porn because it is an addiction and addictions are prisons for the weak of will. I won't be weak neither will I be prisoner to my senses. I want to be strong and I want to be free. So my issue with pornography is neither a moral nor ethical one. For me, it is all about mastering my body and mind through the control of self (all growth starts with the self). The first and best and most immediate way to control the self is via the senses, and I tackled (and continue to tackle) my senses through the deliberate slaughter of my addictions. The Kabbalah teaches us that all our power, all our wealth is locked into our addictions, and when we kill those addictions we win our power back. And when we have our power back we can do anything we like with it.

Those who are heavily addicted are prisoners to their addiction. Killing your addictions opens the door to freedom. (Our main addictions in this society are drugs, alcohol, gambling, pornography and people pleasing. Most people are infected with at least one of these, some people have them all.) It is a trick that I learned from Gandhi, who used this method of abstention to change the course of human history (no less). At the time of his death he had some three hundred million followers. He believed that each of us has one major addiction and that when you closed the door to that one, you closed the door to all your addictions. And when you controlled yourself you literally controlled the world.

This is what my friend the wasp taught me.

Like most people, I convinced myself that a little bit of porn was OK as long as I kept control of it. But with something as powerful as sex (especially for the sexually-profligate male who has about a million years of procreational conditioning in his genes) moderation (I believe) is an untenable philosophy. Like any drug you indulge, each injection needs to be stronger and sooner than the last to get the same buzz. It is small wonder then that people who initially indulge light flirtation with porn quickly progress to the hardcore, often dangerous, mutations that no longer resemble the procreational act of intercourse with a loving partner. I always justified it to myself as 'just something blokes did' until my appetite grew more and more controlling and started to threaten my integrity. It got so that it was difficult for me to walk down the street without checking out (and imagining what I might do with) the curves of every shapely female that happened to pass by. I'd go into book shops to purchase works on philosophy, psychology and spirituality and suddenly find myself in the erotica section flicking though the pages of porn made to look like art. When you find yourself doing things against your own will, you have to start asking yourself a few questions. The question I asked myself was, 'Is this something I can indulge or will it always be an addiction looking for a host?' We all think we can indulge and flirt around the edges of our addictions, but deep down we know that really we can't, because an addiction that is alive is always an addiction that is a threat. Many famous folks have ruined their careers, their health and their relationships because a flirtation with fire set light to their whole lives. I have many friends who have not given their addictions the respect they demand. Their flippancy has (or will) cost them dearly. Some lost their jobs, others their liberty, many their lives. Whilst I am not saying that porn will kill you, I am saying that it will imprison you (whilst letting you think that you are still free).

And this is where the wasp comes in. This is not a metaphor. It is a true story. I sat in my garden drinking a fruit juice and I did what I always do when I need an honest answer. I'd just indulged in a porn fest (even though I really didn't want to) and was feeling… controlled. And weak. Because I no longer felt that I had a choice in the matter. The urge came on. I indulged it. I felt shit afterwards. It had become a habitual cycle. I knew that I wanted to lose this addiction but I just couldn't find enough reason to stop. I kept rationlising and telling myself that 'a little bit won't do you any harm.' Deep down I knew that the little bit was getting bigger and bigger. It needed to be stopped. So I put down the empty glass, closed my eyes and asked for a sign. When I opened my eyes there was a wasp hovering just above my glass. It landed briefly on the glass, stole a residue of my fruit juice and flew away. Within a few brief seconds the wasp was back. He was still being careful; he hovered, landed, had a look around, took a glob of juice from just inside the glass and flew away again. When he returned the third time he was more confident. He flew straight into the glass, took several globs of juice and, when he was ready, flew off. I smiled as I watched the wasp return again and again, each time more confident, each time staying a little longer, each time going a little deeper into the glass and each time drinking in a little more than the last.

Until the final time.

Arrogant now, my wasp flew straight to the bottom of the glass where there was a pool of thick juice. He stood right in the middle of it and drank and drank and – started to drown. He was up to his little knees in juice and could not lift himself back out.

The small indulgence had quickly turned into a life-threatening addiction.

I got the message.

I tipped the glass so that the wasp – having kindly passed on its wisdom to me – could fly away to live another day.

I never indulged my addiction again.

Chapter 20

The Power of Books

To my pleasure, I have discovered the hidden power of books.

What we need to help us rise above the crowd is information. Actually, I stand corrected. I know plenty of people with information by the bucketload but for whatever reason they do not use it. I also know many people who use the information they have, but use it wrongly. Aspiring to achieve wisdom is the correct way to use information. One of the best ways to collect information (and of course inspiration and aspiration) is books. When I spend thousands of pounds on books, I consider it an investment in me, the person most likely to get me where I want to be. In books, we have the opportunity to access the knowledge of a thousand life times and assimilate it until it becomes us. I am the living embodiment of what I have experienced and a big part of what I have experienced has been gained through the medium of reading. I always tell my little lad (when he is struggling to get into a book) that readers are leaders. Small libraries make great men. It is something that I believe emphatically. I have yet to meet a hugely successful person that wasn't a voracious reader. I even took a speed-reading course so that I could get through more material. It's all out there just waiting for you, and if you go to a public library, it's absolutely free.

Can you imagine that, all that knowledge, all the secrets, all that information for the price of a few beers and a curry? I've spent up to £50 on a single book if it was the one that I was looking for. People often say that the only way out of the rat race is through football or sport or pure luck. It's not true. The best way out is through the library. Mention any famous name and I'll almost guarantee that you'll be able to find their whole life – highs, lows, successes, failures, likes and dislikes, and the secrets to their success – between the pages of a library book. Now if that is not offering it all up on a plate for your inspiration, I don't know what is. I find it absolutely incredible that you can go into any bookshop (or even the Internet) and buy the lives of the greatest men and women in history. You can find out why and how single individuals changed the course of history.

One man, William Wallace, witnessed the slaughter of a whole village of people and decided that he was going to do something about it. He told his wife. She said, 'But you're only one man.' That one man changed the course of history with his strength and courage. Have you read about this great and saintly woman, Mother Teresa? She cared for thousands and touched the hearts of millions. Just an ordinary girl who did extraordinary things; a village girl who touched the whole planet. What about the courage of Churchill, the tenacity of Thatcher, the wisdom of the Dalai Lama, the power and love of Sai Baba, the focus and dreams of Bill Gates, the rise and fall of Bonaparte? The list is absolutely endless. And they are all there waiting in books to point you in the right direction. All these extraordinary men and women saying, 'Let me tell you what I've learned in my life.' What an incredible opportunity.

I am sitting here with a book of drawings by Saul Steinberg staring up at me. Steinberg isn't dead; he is alive and kicking in my office. He sat here, alive in his work, saying, 'What can I do for you Geoff? What can I teach you about my life through my work? Ask me, I'm here.' Did you know that Escher lives with me? You're damn right he does! And he only cost me about 20 quid. It was an absolute steal, I have to tell you. A steal. He is here with me now. All his drawings and all his words. When I am feeling a little insecure about my work he is there to help me.

'Listen, Geoff,' he tells me, 'we all feel insecure at times. I went on to become a world-renowned artist but there wasn't a day when I didn't doubt my work. There wasn't a day when I didn't think, "Is this any good?"'

Escher has taught me that insecurity driven into your work is what makes it great. The very fact that the great Escher can doubt his own work, can feel insecure, can feel like giving it all up, makes me feel that I am not on my own and that it is OK to have bad days. An ordinary person can reach the stars. I remember first looking at his work and being filled with awe. I'd never have believed that he would have any insecurities at all about this great art. But in his book he said, 'I've absolutely no reason to moan about the "success" of my work, nor about the lack of ideas for there are plenty of them. And yet I'm plagued by an immense feeling of inferiority, a desperate sense of general failure. Where do these crazy feelings come from?'

I have Gandhi's life story in front of me. The book cost eight pounds. The price was so little that I am almost embarrassed to mention it. I spend more than that on car parking in a single week. Yet this one book has given me more direction and more hope than any amount of money could have. Mr Gandhi has taken me behind the scenes of his life and shown me the rights and the wrongs. He has given me the secret to inner power, he has taught me that faith in yourself and your God means immortality. This also means that nothing is beyond you once you decide to ride the bull. He has shown me that I only have to master one single thing in my life and I can have anything I want. That one single thing is 'me.' Gandhi learned how to lead himself, and he made loads of mistakes along the way. By doing so he built up a personal following of over three hundred million people. Can you imagine that? And reading his book taught me that I could, you could, and we all could do exactly the same thing.

There are only so many things we can learn in one lifetime, only so many lessons we can learn with the finite years that we are allotted. It's not enough time really. That's why books were invented. You can take a thousand great people and learn the lessons they gleaned from their lives. If you discipline yourself and get a lot of reading done, you can become the manifestation of a thousand great people.

Take what it was that made them legendary and make it a part of you. These people have left their stories, their 'instructions for life' so that you can get onto the fast track, so that you don't have to do the thousands of experiments they had to do to learn what they learned. Once you have acquired this knowledge you can use it to power your own journey of discovery. If you wanted to get around London the best thing to do would be to buy a street map.

The biographies of great people are simply that, street maps to life. They have departed to another plane and left you the treasure maps. It's great. It's so wonderful. All you have to do is get out there and buy the books, read the stories, learn the lessons and put them into action.

If you make reading a habit, it'll be the best habit you ever make.

Chapter 21

The Reciprocal Universe

I spoke with a guy the other day who told me that his passion was directing film. He lived and breathed directing. It was all he wanted to do. I knew he was kidding himself. He wasn't directing. He worked a nine-to-five job that bored him completely. He was not a member of any film groups. He did not direct his own films on the weekends. All he did was talk.

Directors do not talk, they direct.

Take Shane Meadows. He wanted to be a director so he got together with a few mates and a camera and directed a bunch of short films that got him noticed. Today he is one of the most respected and sought after directors in Britain.

He wanted to direct so he directed. He did not wait for the grants or the permissions or the favours or the fates. He got a camera, he got his mates and he got busy making films.

That is what directors do.

I have a friend who wants to write. He tells me that he lives and breathes writing. Writing is his life. As soon as his money situation is better, he is going to invest in a course, a computer and maybe a trip to Cannes where he could pitch his film idea and get the funds he needs to sit and write the great work that he has in him. It was only the money that was holding him back, he said.

But it was not the cash that was stopping him. Neither was it the time or the tides. It was simply the fact that he was not a writer because writers write.

Writers do not talk a good script. They sit on their arses and bleed into their computers until they have 120 pages (that will need to be paired painfully down to 90) of carefully crafted prose. Then (after the director, the producer, the actors, the financers, the designer, the tea boy and the runners have read the first draft) they go away and write it again and again and again until it positively shimmers.

I know that my friend is not a real writer because he throws something together over a weekend and blames the fates when it comes back unread and unwanted.

I have another friend (several actually) who wants to make a splash in the world of martial arts. He has something big to say (he says) and the minute the circumstances are right (perhaps next year?) he will say it. He thinks about training in the US with the Machado brothers (but it's too dear). He dreams of going to Brazil to train with the Gracie family (but its too far). He might even do a little stint in Japan (but his wife isn't keen). If only he was as lucky as me and was able to give up his job and train full-time he felt sure that he could hit the world stage.

But he knows deep down (as I know) that the circumstances will never quite favour him. There will never be enough money to purchase tutelage from the Gracies, Brazil will always be too far a trip and his wife will never agree to Japan. And this is not because any of these things are not possible, but because my friend does not really want them enough. He is not really a martial artist with something big to say to the world. He is just a man with a bag of excuses that get ever more diverse and inventive.

Martial artists train, with the best folks on the planet, whenever and wherever they can. They live and they breathe it. They create their own favour, they find the money, the time, the permission. They move with such force that the whole universe is forced to react and create their dream. The universe is touch-sensitive to our intentions. Let me tell you that it does not wait for tomorrow, next week or next year.

It waits only for you.

So let me ask you this: When are you going to make a move? When are you going to command the fates to do your bidding? When are you going to wave your baton of intention and orchestrate the universe? Don't wait like the masses for tomorrow; it does not exist.

Now is the time to act. Book yourself on that directing course you always wanted to do. Start the writing class that has been in your mind forever. Set a deadline date to make your first film. Sit and write, go and run. Whatever it is that you have been dreaming of, make it real now, before you, like the millions before, become the dust of a generation that died with their best music still in them.

And if you are scared, if the very thought of acting makes you quiver with fear; GOOD.

Discomfort is good.

All growth has a kernel of discomfort, a red light for the majority, but for the minority – those with spunk and drive and ambition – discomfort is a green light.

But nothing will move until you move. Nutrients do not mobilise until the seed of intention is planted, fate does not shape circumstance without action, serendipity only manifests when we take up our positions and act.

Jump and a net will appear.

Chapter 22

There is No Land Rover

'There is no Land Rover. There is no Land Rover.
There is… NO LAND ROVER.'

I say it over and over again in my mind with the
rhythm of a metronome.

'There is no Land Rover.'

It keeps me sane. It keeps me on track. It stops me
from being fooled into resting up and celebrating too
soon, loosening my helmet straps before the fight is
won.

'There is no Land Rover. There is no… '

I suppose I should explain what I'm talking about
before you get to thinking that me and my glassy-
smooth marbles have parted company.

Picture the scene. You are on selection for the SAS.
You've just hiked goodness knows how many miles

over the icy, toe-blackening Brecon Beacons on little more than a Mars Bar and the promise that 'when you see the Land Rover, you're home. Jump in the back, take off your boots, have yourself a brew.'

So all the way around, over hills and valleys, past the graves of former aspirants, walking on blisters, working around strains and cuts and injuries, hovering somewhere between breathlessness and total exhaustion, living on fresh air and a frozen chocolate bar, total collapse an ever present vulture on your left shoulder, utter failure an odds-on favourite on your right... and then you see it. Like a watery oasis in a dry desert.

The Land Rover.

Home.

You smile for the first time in days. You quicken your pace. Your mind rushes forward to a hot tea, maybe some food and bed. But just as you get within a few feet of your golden carriage, it drives off leaving you stranded and confused and distraught – and fooled. The sergeant (dressed in a warm coat, sipping a hot tea) tells you to continue on. When you ask him, 'How much further,' he gives you one of those wry smiles and says, 'Until you see the Land Rover.'

Most people, at this point, do not continue on. They take an imaginary towel and throw it into the ring of metaphor. They have been tricked, and (for the majority) that trick is enough to kill their dream.

It has beaten them. They only placed enough fuel in the tank to get them to the Land Rover, and not beyond. Not even a foot beyond. For those who do manage to pick themselves up and continue (for an added and unspecified distance), there is instant enlightenment.

'There is no Land Rover.'

And that becomes their mantra. Until they are literally sitting inside the vehicle of choice with a hot tea, the Land Rover does not exist.

There is no Land Rover.

Especially when everyone around you is telling you that there is.

I remember this every time I think a script is going to be optioned (definitely this time), a battle is going to finish (imminently) or a big deal is as good as done (just 't's to cross and 'i's to dot). I have seen many strong fighters beaten just at the point where they thought victory was certain. I've lost count of friends who have celebrated a deal before that all important eleventh hour. Regretfully, I had friends who lost their lives when they loosened their helmet straps because they believed that the enemy had retreated and the fight was (as good as) won.

So many people fall for the Land Rover trick and give up just short of greatness because they allow themselves to believe that the Land Rover exists. Well, it does exist, sort of, but only when you've got your arse on the seat, and the tea in your hand. Until then is it little more than a phantom. It is healthy to remember this if you intend to reach the top in any game because (believe me) that big deal is always looming. The Land Rover is always 'just over the next hill.'

When the film is on screen, when the cheque is in the bank (and has cleared) and when the back door is bolted and secured, I take my celebratory beverage because that is the only time the Land Rover is real.

Until then there is no Land Rover.

And that will remain my mantra.

Chapter 23

They Laughed at Lowry

Excitedly I phoned a friend to tell him my news. I'd just won an international development award for my film script *Clubbed* (based on my book *Watch My Back*); I had to tell someone. It's what you do when providence lights your day. 'Oh, I see,' he said half-scoffing, half laughing, 'I suppose it'll be the Oscars next then?' His attitude landed like a heavy right. There was bitterness in his tone that made me regret the call.

'Well yea,' I replied (a bit too defensively), 'if that's what I intend to do then why not? Why not! There's a guy in Preston, Nick Park, who's won four!' (If I have to I'll go and get one of his!)

After replacing the receiver, still reeling from his unexpected response, I assured myself that my friend's attitude need not ruin my day, and I should never let him, or any others, hold me back. Criticism, cynicism and jealousy are a familiar trinity, often encountered when leaving a muddy comfort zone en route to a starry ideal. I wasn't the first to be laughed at for daring to dream, neither would I be the last.

When a young German climber told his friends of his bold intentions to climb the perilous mountain Nanga Parbat solo – a feat never before attempted, let alone achieved – they didn't just laugh at him. They called him insane. Equally insane was the idea that two inexperienced men (with an investment of only $30 and a penchant for good ice cream) could one day take on confectionary giant Hagen Das. Reinhold Messner climbed Nanga Parbat solo only six weeks after conquering Everest without oxygen. Ben & Jerry turned their $30 investment into a billion dollar, giant-slaying industry. Who's laughing now?

And they laughed at Lowry, too, you know. When the painter L.S. Lowry first placed his oils to canvas, the haughty elite of the contemporary art world held their chuckling bellies and laughed the gentle northerner out of Manchester. They slandered him at every opportunity for trying to be more than (they thought) he was. They called him an amateur and his work (at best) naïve. 'Who (they asked) does he think he is?' Later, when the (so-called) mighty had crumbled under the might and beauty of Lowry's vision, and his genius shone through the oils (bidders eventually paid millions to own one of his originals), Lowry had the last laugh. His later exhibitions were dedicated to 'the men who laughed at Lowry.' Manchester opened *The Lowry Galleries* to honour his work.

I love that! Don't you love that? All of us have at one time or another had our ideas stamped on, scoffed at or laughed about – often by those closest to us. All of us have watched the uncouth kick our dreams around the floor like cola cans. I love the Lowry story because I have been the butt of many an unkind 'who does he think he is' jibe when I dared to swim against the societal stream. I can take solace in the fact that they laughed at Lowry. He became global, not only in spite of his detractors, but also perhaps because of them.

I can well remember being bored to depression in the distant past and thinking, 'There must be more to life than this.' Seeking answers, I turned to my workmate at the factory – elbow-deep in suds, nails full of shit – and said to him, 'There's got to be more to life than this.' He laughed at me, then leaning forward (as though about to tell me a secret), he winked at me (as wise old veterans are inclined to do), 'This is your lot,' he said, 'you should be grateful. This is a job for life.'

It was the job-for-life bit that scared the tripe out of me. I think he could tell by the way my jaw went slack and my eyes hit the floor like marbles that his shop-floor philosophy had failed to enlighten me. What he said next – not just the words, but the bitterness and conviction with which he delivered them – didn't either. It was like a dry slap across the gob.

'You'll still be here when you're 60.'

Shortly after my tête-à-tête with Plato-of-the-lathe, I snapped my broom (very symbolic) and left the factory forever, never to return. All the things I wanted to do, things I was told I could not – I did. And more. And I am still doing them. This is my life, I can do anything, go anywhere, be whomever I want. We all can. And for those that laugh at my dreams, watch out!

They laughed at Lowry. And look what happened to him.

Chapter 24

Time

My first book was written whilst sitting on the toilet in a factory that employed me to sweep floors, so you can imagine the fun I have when people comment – on finding out that I am a writer – 'Of course I'd love to write a book but I haven't got the time.' Invariably, their faces scrunch into question marks when I ask, 'Is there a toilet where you work?'

Not that I recommend the loo as the healthiest environment to write your latest – or indeed first – bestseller, far from it. In fact, after six months of sitting on the throne writing, I now suffer loss of feeling in my lower legs and a permanent red ring around my bum. I am just making the point that if you have the will you'll always find a way, but if you haven't, or you harbour any doubts or fears, then lack of time will always be a convenient excuse not to live your dreams.

When I wrote my first book I was doing two jobs and bringing up a family. I wanted desperately to write a book. I was fully committed to writing it. And, hey, I found the time. But by the same count, whenever I failed to fully commit myself to a goal – and there were many such occasions – or when I did not place my heart in the driving seat, 'time' was not forthcoming and the vehicle refused to move.

The next convenient excuse (believe me I have used them all) that people lean towards is lack of facility. (Do you have a toilet where you work?) Granted, at some point in your development, tools and facilities will be important and lack of them can hold you back, but that's no excuse for not starting out, and certainly no pretext for not succeeding. Pelé, arguably the greatest football player of all time, honed his ball skill kicking coconuts barefoot (ouch!) on the beach. Many a thriving, multi-million- (even multi-billion-) pound business was started from a rickety garden shed held together by chunks of work ethic and a set of hand-me-down, elbow-greased tools. A great proportion of successful entrepreneurs built their conglomerates out of cottage industry. Many godzillionaires made their fortunes not only despite their handicaps but also because of them. Richard Branson's first office was a public phone booth. He had no facilities and no money, but he did have a forceful desire that attracted success and convinced bank managers to hand over the readies without a security or reference in sight.

Do you realise how many genius ideas are lost when the moment is not seized, and how many are stolen while people stand in the shadow of trepidation? For instance, it is thought that some of the greatest writers of each generation never see their name in print and are never published. And it's not because prospective publishers turn down their work, rather it is because the authors never send their work to them. Or even worse, they never actually write it in the first place.

All my early work was hand-written and in severe conditions that did not lend themselves to my quest. Until I could afford a word processor (later a computer) my working tools consisted of one blue biro (with perfunctory chewed top) and a lined, ring-bound reporter's pad kindly donated by the factory stores. I had no time, no machine with fail-safe grammar and spell check – unless you count my wife who kept saying things like, 'You've spelt that wrong' – and no hefty commission-carrot tempting the words from my often uncooperative unconscious. My only incentive, my driving force, was the dread of having to work in the factory for the rest of my life.

The only thing I did have that set me apart from the crowd was desire. Whilst I may have lacked the contemporary tools of the scribe and my writing quarters were certainly not ideal (one might say that they were piss-poor), I did desperately want to write. My want was always greater than my lack. Once you have desire and you totally commit yourself to the process it is almost as though the whole universe conspires to make it happen. Those who don't make the commitment rarely, if ever, make the grade. And I know how hard it can be. I am sympathetic to family and work commitments. I brought up four children so I know all about responsibility. But as I said, time is very malleable, it can be stretched, it accommodates committed souls, those searching for the grail of achievement. Paradoxically, time can be cruel; it will be gone forever, never to be seen again, if we fail to use it profitably. We immortalise our time when we invest every second, minute and hour in the present.

And I figure that when it comes to using our time we would be wise to recognise that we are all allotted the same amount. Branson and Gates only get 24 hours a day. It is what we do with our time that determines where our lives may lead. For me it means getting up early and going to bed late. It also means sacrificing some of the little things that act as time-eating termites. But above all it means refraining from using the time-honoured excuse, 'I haven't got time' because you have. Really! In my experience, 'haven't-got-the-time' is just a pseudonym for 'haven't-got-the-will'. You'll always fit in more if 'more' is preceded by a no-excuses personal commitment to making it happen. If you want something enough, and I mean really want it with your heart and soul, nothing will stop you, nothing will get in your way.

You don't have to look far to see the people that don't make that commitment. They're the ones sitting in the factory canteen bemoaning their existence and blaming the world for their lack. I was once one of them. Now I make a commitment. For many reasons. Not least because I refuse to be a 90-something coffin dweller spending my days regretting the things that I failed to do.

Chapter 25

Waterfall

You know how it is sometimes. You are going through an emotional stretch and things feel a little (or a lot) dark. You feel sort of needlessly tortured. I figure it is simply a purgatory situated somewhere between the edge of our comfort zones and freedom that we will continue to visit as long as we continue to grow. I do hope so. As uncomfortable as it might be I know that without adversity there will be no advance. And who would want that?

I was there again recently actually. In that dark void. Life had cornered me with a heavy dose of highly-challenging workload and unexpected family illness. I was as vulnerable as the lobster shedding its shell. So I did what I often do between the night and day of personal transformation. I went for a walk in the local country park to see if nature had any lessons to offer, something that might rub a little balm across my throbbing brow. Nature has many lessons. In fact much of what I have learned thus far about pain has been through observing how (as the Bible says) the lilies in the field neither spin nor toil.

But today nature was not forthcoming. Nothing I observed offered any solace. Until, that is, I hit the last five minutes of my walk and stood on a bridge that acted as both a crossing point to a small stream and an observation platform to a beautiful little waterfall. It had been raining heavily all week and, as a consequence, the waterfall was gushing over the precipice into the stream below. The turmoil of the fall seemed to exactly mirror the internal struggle that I was experiencing, raging and seemingly uncontrollable emotions that were racing through my mind and body with an energy that I did not recognise as my own. Then I intuited something else, something that gave me the inspiration that I was looking for.

I noticed that in the stream immediately after the fall the water was very deep. In fact the deepest part of the whole stream was right there. Immediately after the fall. I liked this observation. It helped me to realise and understand that after adversity, the Niagara that all of us experience during difficult times, a deeper more profound understanding could be found. I stretched back in my mind and realised that my greatest life lessons thus far, the reference points that helped me to negotiate ever new and ever burgeoning challenges, had always been born out of hard times. The good stuff that I wrote about in my books, talked about in my videos/podcasts and dramatised in my films and plays was the fruit of the hard harvests that life had given me. Then I looked further along the stream, on the other side of the bridge, and I noticed that the water there was very calm. This told me something too. It told me that even the most violent storms do not last forever, and that after adversity there is always peace; after great darkness comes great light. This gave me hope. At the time I desperately needed it. Often when we are in the very middle of a crisis our pain feels infinite and without end. My observations told me that no single feeling can last forever. As I continued to watch (and this is completely true) I noticed a duck swimming down the stream. It didn't seem to notice that about ten feet in front of it the waterfall was at full rage. I wondered how the duck might deal with it. I watched and observed and was amazed to see that a few feet away from the waterfall the duck simply lifted itself out of the water, flew above the waterfall and landed safely on the other side of the bridge where the waters were calm. Amazing. What I loved about this was the fact that the raging waterfall was still there, the duck just chose to rise above it. It did not attach to the turmoil below.

I walked away with my first smile in weeks, determined to no longer attach to my pain, knowing that my understanding would deepen because of my experience and that there was a heavy dose of calm coming my way sometime soon.

Chapter 26

We Are All Dying

I have some good news and some bad news for you (as the joke goes). The bad news – and I'm very sorry to be the bearer – is that we are all dying. It's true. I've checked it out. In fact, I've double- and triple-checked it. I've had it substantiated and, well, there's no easy way to say it, we are dying. It's something that I always kind of knew, but never really chose to think about too much. But the fact is, within the next 70 or 80 years – depending on how old you are and how long you last – we are all going to be either coffin dwellers or trampled ash in the rose garden of some local cemetery. We may not even last that long. After all, we never quite know when the hooded, scythe-carrying, bringer-of-the-last-breath might come-a-calling. It could be sooner than we'd like. I have watched death from the sidelines, quite recently in fact, and nothing underlines the uncertainty and absolute frailty of humanity like the untimely exit of a friend.

Scary.

Now that I have depressed you, here's the good news. Knowing that we are all budding crypt-kickers takes away all the uncertainty of life. We already know how the story ends. The prologue and epilogue are already typed in. All that's left is the middle bit and that's down to us. We get to choose the meat of the story.

So, all those plans that you have on the back burner, you know, the great things you're going to do with your life 'when the time is right?' Well, the time is never quite right, I find. It needs to be brought forward and done now, this minute, pronto, in a hurry, as quick as your little legs will carry you. The novel that you want to write, the trip to the Grand Canyon you've always planned to take, your mind's-eye dream-job, the West End play you want to direct – you have to do them now. We're dying, see. It's official.

So putting your dreams on the back burner until the circumstances are right means that they'll probably never be realised. Our only regrets in life are the things we don't do. We owe it to ourselves to go out and do them now before it's too late. Tomorrow? It's all a lie; there isn't a tomorrow. There's only a promissory note that we are often not in a position to cash. It doesn't even exist. When you wake up in the morning it'll be today again and all the same rules will apply. Tomorrow is just another version of now, an empty field that will remain so unless we start planting some seeds. Your time, which is ticking away as we speak (at about 60 seconds a minute chronologically; a bit faster if you don't invest your time wisely) will be gone and you'll have nothing to show for it but regret and a rear-view mirror full of 'could haves', 'should haves' and 'would haves'.

Have you ever noticed when you go to a buffet restaurant how they give you a bowl the size of a saucer and then say, 'Have as much salad as you like but you can only go up once.' Life is like that small salad bowl. Like the hungry people waiting for their main course, we can cram as much into that tiny bowl as we can carry. I love watching people ingeniously stack the cucumber around the side of the bowl – like they're filling a skip – and then cramming it so high that they have to hire a fork-lift truck to get it back to the table. They're not greedy. They just know that they only have one shot at it.

Fill your bowl. We come this way but once so let's make the best of the short stay. Like the once-a-year holiday to Florida or Spain. Fit as much into the short time there as you can. Make sure that you go back home knackered because you got so much done.

If you don't want to be a postman then don't be a postman. Give it up and be a painter, a writer, a tobogganist, whatever. Just don't be something that you patently do not want to be.

And now is the time, not tomorrow. There is no time like the present. If you can't have what you want this very second the least you can do is start the journey now, this minute, while the inspiration is high. We all have the same amount of minutes, we all get the same 24 hours as Branson and Gates. It's just what we do with our time, how we invest it, that determines where our lives may lead.

So what I'm thinking is (and this is not molecular science) if we are dying and our allotted time is finite, why the hell aren't we doing all the things we want to do NOW? What's all this back-burner stuff? And why are we all waiting for the right time when we already know that the right time isn't going to show? The right time is the cheque that's permanently in the post, it never arrives. It's the girl who keeps us standing at the corner of the co-op looking like a spanner. No amount of clock watching will change the inevitable. She's stood us up.

We wait; the right time never arrives.

So I say stop waiting and meet providence half way. Start filling your life with the riches on offer so that when the reaper arrives, you'll have achieved so much, crammed your time so full that he'll fall asleep waiting for your life to flash before your eyes.

Act now or your time will elapse and you'll end up as a sepia-coloured relative that no one can put a name to in a dusty photo album.

Better to leave a biography as thick as a whale omelette than an epitaph.

'Joe Smith... hmmm. He didn't do much did he?'

Chapter 27

What do You Want to do?

I had a letter today from a friend. He was feeling a little sorry for himself (it's allowed – he is human) because he woke up one morning recently and realized why he'd been feeling so depressed for the last month or so. He was living without a purpose. Not that he'd never had a purpose, rather he'd had one and (somehow) lost it. It is easily done. My friend had once courted high aspirations; he was going to train in multi-disciplines and become a martial arts maverick, treading the world stage with the greats. He wanted (he told me) to be the best at something.

Being the funny guy that everyone knows I am I could easily have offered the hilarious advice I give most people who have lost something important. 'Why not look down the back of the settee?'

It is amazing what you can find if you move a few pillows and slide your fingers and wrist into that scary abyss. But from the gloomy tone of my friend's correspondence I figured that even a jokester as original as I might be wasting time with mirth when wisdom (and a quick solution) was being sought to the age-old problem: How do I find my purpose? How can I become the best at something?

In his email, my friend included a list of all the things that he had tried and not completed (this is part of the self-pity. 'Poor me, look at what a failure I am.' I've been here a hundred times myself), he talked about how well his partner was doing with her career, and how he was moving jobs and cities to support her (because he loved her) and also how pleased he was for her success. He also included a list of jobs he quite fancied doing, work that he thought might make 'a great career,' and perhaps one of them might even be the thing he could be the best at.

What he didn't include on his list was what he REALLY wanted to do.

I am not talking about what he thinks he should do or what others think he should do, or what is expected of him. I wasn't interested in what will earn him the most money or even what might offer the 'I've-made-it' status that so many people crave.

In the whole scope of things none of this is important. In colloquial speak, 'It's all bollocks.'

What I really wanted to know, and what I asked him (and what I now ask you) is this: WHAT DO YOU REALLY WANT TO DO? I mean REALLY.

Forget expectation. Forget income. Forget responsibilities. Forget what others want and expect and demand. Forget society, forget the government. Forget what you think and are told is impossible. What do you really want to do? If money and people were not an issue what is it that you would most like to spend your entire waking life doing? What is it that you love so much that time disappears when you do it? What is it that puts a light in your eyes at the mere mention of its name?

That (I told him, I tell you, I tell me) is what he should either be doing or at the very least making plans to do. No more and no less.

A job with great career prospects and great money has nothing whatsoever to do with following a dream. I have friends on six- and seven-figure incomes who hate the jobs that they do with a passion. They tell me that their life/job/family/commitments/mortgage keeps them imprisoned.

I tell them they are wrong. It is their ignorance that keeps them imprisoned.

I tell them that their right to choose differently will set them free.

Consider this: You spend two-thirds of your waking life at work. Do you really want to be bartering that much of your time just for a lifestyle? And anyway, who says you can't earn just as much money and enjoy just as good a lifestyle in a career that you love? I know millionaire plumbers, rich poets, wealthy martial artists.

If you are the best at what you do (and it is easier to be the best when you are passionate about what you do) the money will follow – it always follows passion.

It is at this point that people usually shake their heads and arch an eyebrow (as though I really don't get it) and say something like, 'I've got a mortgage to pay. I've got people relying on me. It is not that easy.'

To which I usually reply, 'I don't remember saying that it was easy. Only that it was possible.'

Of course it's difficult. If it was easy everybody would be doing it. And anyway, if everything came easy what would be the point? I have found that there is no flavour where there is no labour. What you work and strive for has a taste and texture that are only born from effort. I used to work full time as a martial-arts instructor. It was my job to train for a living. And I did train. When I did my 40 rounds on the bag after a five-mile run, a cup of tea was not just a cup of tea. It was a cup of tea! The taste, the texture, the smell, the feel – it was almost miraculous. Similarly, when I got my black belt in judo after some of the hardest training in my life, and certainly the most difficult grading I've ever done, I was a changed man. The lad that walked into the sports centre for the grading on Saturday morning was not the man who emerged on Saturday afternoon.

So hard is where it is at. It is the prerequisite to success. All those who walk around it, walk under it or over it, those that avoid 'hard' like it is a piece of shit on the floor, never get invited to the Emperor's banquet. They sit outside and (many of them) bitch about how the people inside got a lucky break, had it easy, knew someone on the inside (because, as we all know, 'it's who you know'). They wine because they feel overlooked, undervalued, hard-done-by or elbowed out. Or they claim that the person on the inside sold out. And the only reason they themselves didn't make it was because they maintained their integrity.

How noble.

And what a heap of horseshit.

This is the excuse offered by the people who just don't step up. How do I know? I have used the same excuse many times on my way to where I am now. And it wasn't until I buried that sickly heap of self-pity that I finally got on.

If you are good enough you make it. End of story. If you don't make it you look back into your self and take responsibility for that failing and either try again or quit bitching.

Back to my friend. He had lost his purpose. He wanted to find it again. He also wanted to be the best at something, though he was unsure of what that something might be. He was asking for my advice.

What I have learned from my 46-years of life is that anyone can be the best at anything if they are prepared to invest themselves in it (my book *Shapeshifter* has more on this process). To be the very best though, world class, global, I would say that four elements need to be in place.

1) First you need to acknowledge where you are right now. You need to do a brutal inventory of your level. This is important. I know many people (especially in the martial arts) who already think that they are world class and are constantly wondering why the world is not acknowledging them. I remember looking at one of my friends, a decent fighter with a whole heap of potential who wasn't taking that next step. It wasn't happening for him and I couldn't work out why. I said to Sharon, 'This guy has got so much potential. He could be world class. I can't work out what is holding him back.' She looked at him and said said to me, 'He thinks he is world class already.' She was so right. How was he ever going to try for the next level when he thought that he was already there?

So, give yourself an honest check-up. Don't inflate your ability and don't be self-depreciating. Where are you really? If you are not sure (and this is a hard one) ask the one person in your life who will tell you honestly. This needs to be someone that you trust, someone who is not afraid to tell you that you are great, but at the same time is not afraid to tell you that you are just not cutting it. A very famous drummer was approached by his teenage son. 'Dad,' he said, 'I am going to be a world-class drummer.' His dad looked at him and said, 'Then you'd better get busy because at the moment you just ain't doing the work, son.' The reply was harsh and to the point but this is the kind of honesty that you need if you want to be great. Once you have a realistic assessment of where you stand on the hierarchical ladder, you have to make sure the second element is in place.

2) You need an absolute passion for your subject matter. Finding a passion is often difficult for many people because while they want to do something great, they can't always work out what. From my experience, the 'what' in question is probably and usually something that you have always wanted to do since you were a child and would be prepared to do even if there was no money involved. If your purpose is not clear, a search is in order, usually the kind of search that goes in and not out. But if you are really serious about finding purpose don't worry, it'll find you when you are ready.

3) Once you have your purpose in place make sure that it is something that you personally believe you

can be the best at. If you are not sure that you can, maybe you feel too old, too young, too weak or too poor to make the top tier. Scan the book shops and Internet for proof to the opposite. Experience has told me that anyone can do anything. You don't have to look far for sterling examples of people who have achieved the most outrageous success, despite all the elements.

4) Ironically, if you want to aim high, what you do needs to be something that, eventually, you can earn a living from because to be the best at anything you need to work at it full time.

Once you have your four elements in place, it is about making that talk 'walk.' And walk. And walk. Many people talk about being the best at this and that. The martial artists talk about Lee or O'Neil, the guitarists talk Clapton or Hendrix, the screenwriters talk about Abbot or Webb Peoples but when you look closely that is all they do. They talk. And talking doesn't make a champion.

It is about reading it, writing it, watching it, hearing it, seeing it, feeling it, smelling it, talking it (but not too much talking). It is about taking it to bed with you and waking up with it on the tip of your tongue, eating it with your breakfast, supping it through the froth of your beer. It is about surrounding yourself with it and above all else it is about putting in the (thousands of hours of) practise (under escalating instruction) that is needed before the world stage offers you its boards to tread.

Beware. Aiming for pinnacles is uncomfortable. There is hardly any air up there in the higher echelons and you can suffer.

But that's good.

You will never be a great anything if you haven't suffered. Be worthy of the suffering and the struggle, so that when you arrive and people come to you for advise and complain about how hard their life is and how they are struggling, you can say, 'Hey, let tell you about struggle! I remember the time when...'

So, if like my friend you have lost your purpose, retrace your steps to a time when you were inspired, pick up the old scent and make a great adventure out of finding your purpose. If you want to be the best, stop talking and start doing. If this is a time of confusion for you, a time of struggle, get excited because that alone makes this is a great time. Confusion and struggle are the pre-cursers to major breakthroughs.

The universe is in dire need of adventurers and it is waiting for your contribution. Don't let it down.

Chapter 28

Who am I to be a Success?

I've had a few interesting conversations recently with people who really want to achieve some major goals in their lives but are plagued by a false belief that what it is they are aiming for is somehow not possible. 'And even if it is,' they say to me, 'who am I to be a success?'

I have lost count of the amount of times I have heard this comment (and even said the very same thing to myself in my darker moments). My heart goes out to all of those out there inflicted by this dreadful disease we call self-doubt. I know how debilitating it can be and I really do know how you feel.

It might help to know that you are not alone.

Most accomplished people feel this way at one time or another, often even after major successes. They just learn to override the negative voices in their heads and do the work anyway.

It took me a long time to believe in myself, but the more you push through the doubts and the more success you get behind you, the easier it gets. It helps to have some strong points of reference to fall back on. This entails getting a series of (even small) successes behind you to build on.

The great artist Escher was so full of insecurity and self-doubt that he would often feel an almost overpowering urge to stop a project, sometimes as soon as five minutes after starting. He learned to recognise this self-doubt as a pre-curser to all his great works. Because he recognised it he was able to step through it like a fog. He became massively successful not because he never felt doubt or fear, rather he was a success because he learned to ignore, and even use his fears as a fuel. Even the master Samurai on the battlefield is not without fear. His body still sweats and shivers with the anticipation of war, but he sets himself above his biology and steps into the arena not just despite his fear, but perhaps because of it.

It is inspiring to know that even the master feels the same pain and fear as you. But knowing is not enough – you have to 'do.'

Reading and listening will help you learn the process but the only true knowledge is earned knowledge. Loads of people have the facts. A plethora of folks can quote you book, line and verse on how to be the best 'this and that' on the planet, but information without experience is (what Shakespeare might have called) 'a giant's robe on a dwarfish thief.'

So when people ask me for lessons in becoming (for instance) a writer I always say the first lesson in writing is to write. The same as the first lesson of running is to run and the first lesson of fighting is to fight.

It is not the art of knowing, it is the art of doing.

So to be a writer just keep writing. Expect the fear, write anyway. Expect trepidation, set-backs, knock-backs, criticism, put-downs, depression, despair and the occasional failure. Once you have 'made it' expect the same again, when even your biggest fans call you all sorts of horrible names if your second book doesn't measure up (in their eyes) to your first or if you change style of try something new.

The critics lauded JD Salinger when he wrote the classic *Catcher in the Rye*. The very same critics savaged him when his second book was not to their liking. Salinger never published again.

Expect discomfort, it is the pre-requisite. All the gold is in the pain.

Remember this when you try to change in order to grow and the people who love you turn their love to hate because you go from writing articles to books, books to novels, novels to films or films to plays. They liked you as you were and where you were. Remember this when you try to change styles or systems or dogmas and the frightened and the wary warn you to 'leave well enough alone.' If you want to be anything – a writer, martial artist, tinker, tailor, soldier, sailor – more than the norm, I can tell you now that you have chosen a very difficult path. I applaud you for it because difficult in the game of life is categorically a green light and not a red. You have to be able to greet fear and doubt and (at times) utter despair along your chosen path and face these demons down.

Who are you to succeed?

Who the fuck are you not to?

You may deem great success an impossible thing, but it is not, nothing is. I have lost count of the number of people who told me that I was kidding myself when I said I wanted to become a top martial artist and when I said I was going to write books and films. Close friends. Even people that I loved scoffed at me. That is why I was so elated at the BAFTAs because it proved to all of them (and to myself) that I (and they) can do anything.

Everything you want resides just behind that membrane of fear you are feeling right now. To get the gold, you have to get past the fear.

Chapter 29

You Are What You Ingest

Have you noticed how many programmes there are on the telly these days about healthy eating? Everything from *Jamie's Dinners* to Dr Gillian McKeith's *You Are What You Eat*. I love it. I do. I think it's long overdue. We've all known (or at least we have always been told) that the food we take in determines the performance we give out. We also know (or should anyway) that the leading cause of death (heart disease) finds its way in through bad eating habits. If this is the case – and the evidence for it is compelling – why do so many people still continue to eat a diet of poison ivy and expect rose-petal health? Why (as the old adage goes) do we do what we do when we know what we know?

This is a question I am going to leave you to ponder on. Mostly because the answer is as obvious as your nose. It is not physical food that I find completely intriguing, it is cerebral food.

I have spent most of my life reviewing and studying diet in my search for self-improvement (if not enlightenment) and through years of trial and error I managed to get my diet pretty tight. I have to say that I did feel a lot better for it. Energy was up, health was up, performance improved, mood found a steady and happy homeostasis. But even with my food in place there was still something missing. There was still a piece of the jigsaw lost. It was at this point I had a great realisation. You can get your diet as tight as you like and it still will not bring you optimum results if your thoughts aren't right. Don't get me wrong. Healthy eating improves thinking no end, but to take your thoughts to an Olympic level you need to start watching your cerebral diet. Thinking comes through and from the brain, and the brain has several forms of nutrition, the mainstay being information. This is not a statement of metaphor. Information is a literal food for the brain, it relies upon it for growth, and whether that growth is healthy or not depends entirely upon the quality of your information ingested. In fact every piece of information that you absorb becomes chemicals in your body. Watch a porn flick or a violent movie and the body will explode with a cocktail of stress hormones looking for a fuck or a fight, and if it doesn't get one (of either) those same hormones will quickly turn rogue. Watch a movie about Gandhi or have a conversation about the global power of love with Mother Teresa and you'll be filled with endorphins and probably want to save a small village in India or tell someone close that you love them.

Your daily diet of cerebral grub consists of what you watch on TV, listen to on the radio, read, who you talk to (this includes talking to yourself), hang out with, marry, admire and mimic. Stand with gangsters and you'll get the violent high-octane kick of adrenalin that makes you want to set up a business in the dark arts. Have an afternoon with Deepak Chopra and you'll probably want to study metaphysics and manifest your dreams out of mid-air. Spend the evening having it large with the pub cynics and you may doubt the very existence of good by the end of the evening. Have an afternoon with BJJ maverick John B. Will and you'll be inspired to traverse the globe – like he has – in search of great martial mentors. Even your environment feeds your brain. If you are in a shitty part of the city under constant threat of attack don't believe for even a second that it will not feed your brain. But is this the kind of nutrition that you want?

I am telling you all this but you know it already. If you have been around for even two decades you will have experienced enough to know that influences influence. And if they are strong influences they influence strongly.

Here's the good news and the bad news. Good news first. Like physical diet, cerebral diet can be changed. Your environment and influences, what you watch and read and who you talk to can be changed in the beat of a healthy heart.

If you have the foresight and the courage.

Bad news. Like physical diet, cerebral nutrition needs to be consistent. The good results only last as long as the good information. It needs to be topped-up daily until it is habit. One bad day on a food binge can throw you into a state of nutritional crisis (your organs are high priority, you only get the one set). Equally, one bad night of poor choice company could throw you in jail or worse. The mortuary slab has no respect for prior good behaviour.

I have seen many a good soul made obese simply because of greedy and poor-choice eating. I have seen many a good soul turn gangrenous simply because of poor-choice friends.

So I say be very fussy about what you ingest. Everything that goes in will come out in a similar fashion. If you don't want to see the replay of bad health for the rest of your life, get your bollocks on the table and make the changes. Stop pretending that what you eat and who you sit with doesn't affect the very foundation of who you are.

You are what you ingest. So ingest what you want to be.

The Elephant and The Twig
The Art of Positive Thinking

Geoff Thompson

£9.99 P/b

ISBN: 1-84024-264-7
ISBN 13: 978-1-84024-264-5

In India, young elephants are trained in obedience by being tied to an immovable object like a tree. No matter how hard the baby elephant pulls it cannot break free, and eventually, after trying to break away and being thwarted time and again, it believes that it cannot escape, no matter what it does. Ultimately, a fully-grown adult weighing several tons can be tied to a twig and won't even try to escape.

Do you ever feel that you are tied to an immovable object and can't break free? That you couldn't possibly give that presentation, that you would never be able to go it alone in business, or that you have to remain stuck in a social and lifestyle rut as there is no other alternative? This book argues that what ties you down and prevents you from realising your potential is only a 'twig'. Geoff guides you through the process of breaking the negative thinking that binds us and reveals the '14 Golden Rules to Success and Happiness'.

Shape Shifter
Transform Your Life in 1 Day

Geoff Thompson

£7.99 P/b

ISBN: 1-84024-444-5
ISBN 13: 978-1-84024-444-1

What if you could become anything you wanted? What if there was a method of practice that allowed ordinary men and women to transform themselves into beings of extraordinary talent?

It is a commonly held belief that the leading lights of society are gifted from birth or just plain lucky, but Geoff Thompson believes that anyone with average ability and a strong desire can succeed in any chosen field. The ex-bouncer and factory floor sweeper, now a martial arts expert, screenwriter, Bafta-award winning film-maker and author of 30 books, knows this better than most. In *Shape Shifter*, the first self-help guide of its kind, you will learn:

- That shape shifting is our birthright as a creative species

- How to practise the art of personal transformation, step by step

- That with the right strategy and approach, success is always a choice

www.summersdale.com
www.geoffthompson.com